An Otago Storeman in Solomon Islands

The diary of William Crossan, copra trader, 1885–86

AN OTAGO STOREMAN IN SOLOMON ISLANDS

The diary of William Crossan, copra trader, 1885–86

Edited by

Tim Bayliss-Smith
Reader in Pacific Geography,
University of Cambridge,
Cambridge,
England, UK

and

Judith A. Bennett
Professor of History,
University of Otago,
Dunedin,
New Zealand Aotearoa

E PRESS

Published by ANU E Press
The Australian National University
Canberra ACT 0200, Australia
Email: anuepress@anu.edu.au
This title is also available online at http://epress.anu.edu.au

---

National Library of Australia Cataloguing-in-Publication entry

Title: An Otago storeman in Solomon Islands : the diary of William
            Crossan, copra trader, 1885-86 / edited
            by Tim Bayliss-Smith and Judith A.
            Bennett.

ISBN: 9781922144201 (pbk.) 9781922144218 (ebook)

Subjects: Crossan, William.
            Copra industry--Solomon Islands--History.
            Merchants--New Zealand--Biography.
            New Zealand--History--19th century.
            Solomon Islands--History--19th century.

Other Authors/Contributors:
            Bayliss-Smith, Tim.
            Bennett, Judith A., 1944-

Dewey Number: 993.02

All rights reserved. No part of this publication may be reproduced, stored in a retrieval system or transmitted in any form or by any means, electronic, mechanical, photocopying or otherwise, without the prior permission of the publisher.

Cover design and layout by ANU E Press

This edition © 2012 ANU E Press

Contents

List of Figures vii

Acknowledgements. ix

Introduction: Islands traders and trading 1

1. William Crossan 7

2. Makira islanders and Europeans 15

3. Chiefs and traders 27

4. Crossan's Hada Bay Diary 37

Appendix 1. 'My Dearest Aunt'. 85

Appendix 2. 'All goods at the time of arrival...'. 89

References 91

List of Figures

1. Map of Solomon Islands in 1885.	4
2. The grave of William Moffatt, father of William Crossan, in Whroo, Victoria, Australia.	8
3. Portrait found within the William Crossan diary-notebook, and presumed to depict the author.	9
4. Map of Arosi district and adjacent parts of Makira Island.	16
5. Hada Bay as depicted by Cecil Foljambe.	17
6. Photograph of a man spearing fish and fishing stands at Heuru, 1906.	20
7. Photograph of David Boo, 1906.	21
8. The beach at Heuru, north coast of Arosi District, 1906.	22
9. The schooner *Glencairn*, 62 tons.	23
10. The top-sail schooner *Fearless*, 100 tons.	28
11. A photograph entitled 'Natives at Fatuaa, 1889' found inside the Crossan diary-notebook.	38

Acknowledgements

We are grateful to the Hocken Library, Dunedin for their permission to reproduce an edited version of William Crossan's diary (Misc-MS-1224), the enclosed images, as well as the image of the ship *Fearless*. We also thank the Timuru Port Authority for permission to use this image of the *Fearless*, the Oxley Library, Brisbane for the image of the *Glencairn*, and Bishop Terry Brown for Beattie photographs. The assistance of Janey Jackson in getting copies of records in Bendigo, Australia and, with Anne Forden, in locating and photographing the grave of William Moffat is much appreciated, as is the advice of Sam Alasia. Thanks too go to Doug Munro for his suggestion of an extended introduction and to cartographer, Philip Stickler, Department of Geography, University of Cambridge for the maps.

Tim Bayliss-Smith thanks the University of Otago for a De Carle fellowship in 2010 when he was able to do some research on this project. Judy Bennett is grateful to the Department of History, University of Otago for its constant support, especially the work of Peter Cadogan who assisted with layout. She thanks St John's College, Cambridge for an overseas visiting scholarship so she could begin collaborative work with Tim Bayliss-Smith.

We both thank The Australian National University for its help and guidance in this publication which we hope will be of interest not only to researchers but also the people of Makira, Solomon Islands and Otago, South Island, New Zealand.

Tim Bayliss-Smith and Judy Bennett

Cambridge, England and Dunedin, New Zealand, 2012

Introduction: Islands traders and trading

Solomon Islands in the 1880s

In early September 1885 William Crossan from Otago Province in the South Island of New Zealand arrived at Makira in the Solomon Islands to begin a copra trading enterprise (Figure 1). He left there in early March, 1886, so his stay was a brief six months. He was one of several traders, mainly from Australia, the United States and New Zealand, who began to venture into the Western Pacific from the 1840s. They followed in the wake of itinerant American whalers who had revealed the range of tropical products of value to the West. The earliest traders sought profitable cargoes of bêche de mer and sandalwood destined for the Chinese market. However, the sandalwood was all but cut out by the mid 1860s, so traders turned to a range of other products.[1]

With burgeoning urban populations in industrialising Europe, demand for vegetable oils grew in the late 1860s. Copra - the dried oil-rich kernel of the coconut - proved valuable for soap and candle making. Coconut palms grew naturally throughout the coastal areas of the tropics and needed no tending. The late 1870s and early 1880s were a boom period for copra and certain other products, such as turtle shell, ivory nuts from the sago palm (*Metroxylon* spp.), trochus shell, mother of pearl shell and bêche de mer. In the later decades of the century several traders in these goods lived in the islands on a semi-permanent basis. Some took their produce directly to major metropolitan ports such as Sydney, Australia or Auckland, New Zealand while others were agents for major trading houses mainly in these centres. All traders relied on colonial shipping, some from these ports but some also from bases in Fiji, which became a British colony in 1874. Others had links with German firms, mainly based in Samoa.[2]

The Solomon Islands group was a source of these tropical products, but it also exported labour. Underway in the 1870s, the overseas labour trade took, by force or persuasion, thousands of Solomon Islanders mainly to Fiji and Queensland but also to Samoa and New Caledonia. They worked on cotton, sugar-cane and coconut plantations, on farms and in mines, and they were away for at least one three-year period. Once abroad, the islanders quickly learned the value of trade goods, such as steel axes and knives, cloth, tobacco, muskets and rifles. Certainly by the 1880s, island traders could count on these returnees from the

---
1 Dorothy Shineberg, *They Came for Sandalwood: A Study of the Sandalwood Trade in the South-West Pacific, 1830-1865* (Melbourne: Melbourne University Press, 1967).
2 Peter Biskup, ed., *The New Guinea Memoirs of Jean Baptiste Octave Mouton* (Canberra: The Australian National University, 1974), 21-22.

colonies as eager customers who sometimes could even be recruited as local agents for trading. Their growing addiction to imported tobacco was another way in which islanders became increasingly dependent on foreign goods.

The example of the returned labourers added to the desires and demands of their stay-at-home kinsfolk who also began to seek out the traders. Some Solomon Islanders on the large high islands, however, had limited contact with these outside influences because, from the days of early whalers' visits, the coastal or salt water people had largely monopolised contact with the newcomers. In much of Melanesia the coastal or salt water peoples were usually at odds with their inland or bush neighbours except at set trading sites when bush women exchanged localised produce, such as taro bartered for fish from the coastal women, all under the watchful eyes of their armed menfolk.[3] Occasionally, clan relationships or marriage links could be a passport for a bush man to slip safely through to the coast to offer himself to a recruiting ship as labour for overseas plantations, but the return route three to six years later might well be blocked because of shifting alliances and village sites.[4] With traders at particular locations, inland men could afford to wait for an opportunity to negotiate secure access.

The bulk of the traders in the Solomon Islands worked as agents for Sydney firms, which supplied them with goods and sailing vessels and sent ships fairly regularly to collect the produce. In regard to copra, from 1900 it found a ready buyer in Lever Brothers Sydney's soap factory at Balmain or was re-exported to Britain for processing. Good returns meant more production as well as more competition, to the extent that by the time William Crossan came to Makira, the metropolitan prices paid for copra were falling. Yet those who actually resided in the Solomons for long periods were few – in 1870 about seven, in 1880 about six and in 1885 around ten. Temporary residents like Crossan were more numerous, from twelve to twenty in any one year between 1877-1893.[5]

For strangers, life in the Solomon Islands as well as most of the rest of Western Melanesia could be dangerous and often unpredictable because there was no centralised colonial administration until late in the century, and even then it had only partial control. Although the Western Pacific High Commissioner, based in Fiji, had certainly extra-territorial authority over British subjects from 1877, the annual appearance of one or two itinerant British warships did little for the everyday security of foreigners in the Solomon Islands. Indigenous politics were complicated and highly localised, and the cultures of the region

---

3   John Cromar, *Jock of the Islands* (London: Faber & Faber, 1935), 150-151, 339; Elisabeth Krämer-Bannow, *Among the Art-Loving Cannibals of the South Seas*. Trans Waltraud Schmidt, (Adelaide: Crawford House, 2009), 92-94.
4   Judith A Bennett, *Wealth of the Solomons: A History of a Pacific Archipelago, 1800-1978* (Honolulu: University of Hawai'i Press, 1987),78-87; Krämer-Bannow, *Among the Art-Loving Cannibals*, 47-49.
5   Bennett, *Wealth of the Solomons*, 59-60.

were diverse, with groups often in conflict. The more permanent traders who survived were those who allied themselves with a local leader or 'big man', and in time they often married indigenous women, as well as establishing good relations with native agents in more distant locations.

All such alliances, however, were subject to a background of pressures that a newcomer, unfamiliar with the language and history, could hardly imagine. In addition, traders were highly competitive among themselves, soon offering higher prices or superior goods to the local people. Some were not above cheating each other should the opportunity arise. But sooner or later, whether he was trader or labour recruiter, those who tried to cheat Solomon Islanders were very likely to come off second best. Even if they managed to escape, indigenous retribution might be visited on the next unsuspecting white man who was handy. Riddled with pitfalls, this was the shifting political and commercial landscape that foreigners such as Crossan had to negotiate. All foreigners, whether they were itinerant missionaries, traders or the occasional visiting 'naturalist' also had to deal with a range of tropical diseases, the most common being malaria.[6] These islands were no paradise for the white man.

The Solomon Islands became a British Protectorate in 1893, and eventually in 1896 a small administrative presence was established on Tulagi in the Florida Islands (Ngella), north of Guadalcanal. It did not make much impact in 'pacifying' the Solomon Islanders until the first decade of the twentieth century. By then, the day of the 'old time copra dealers' was nearing its end, not only in the Solomons but also in much of the Western Pacific. Only a few traders persisted, combining trading with recruiting labour for new plantation development within the archipelago. Trade with local copra producers certainly continued often via native or Chinese agents, but with the establishment of copra plantations it became mainly a profitable side-line for the incoming planters as well as for mercantile and shipping firms such as Burns Philp, with its network of well-supplied stores and fast steamship service from Australia.[7]

---

6 Bennett, *Wealth of the Solomons*, 69-72.
7 Bennett, *Wealth of the Solomons*, 102-124, 201-209: Biskup, *The New Guinea Memoirs*, 24-28; Krämer-Bannow, *Among the Art-Loving Cannibals*, 17, 22, 45, 76, 158, 170, 229.

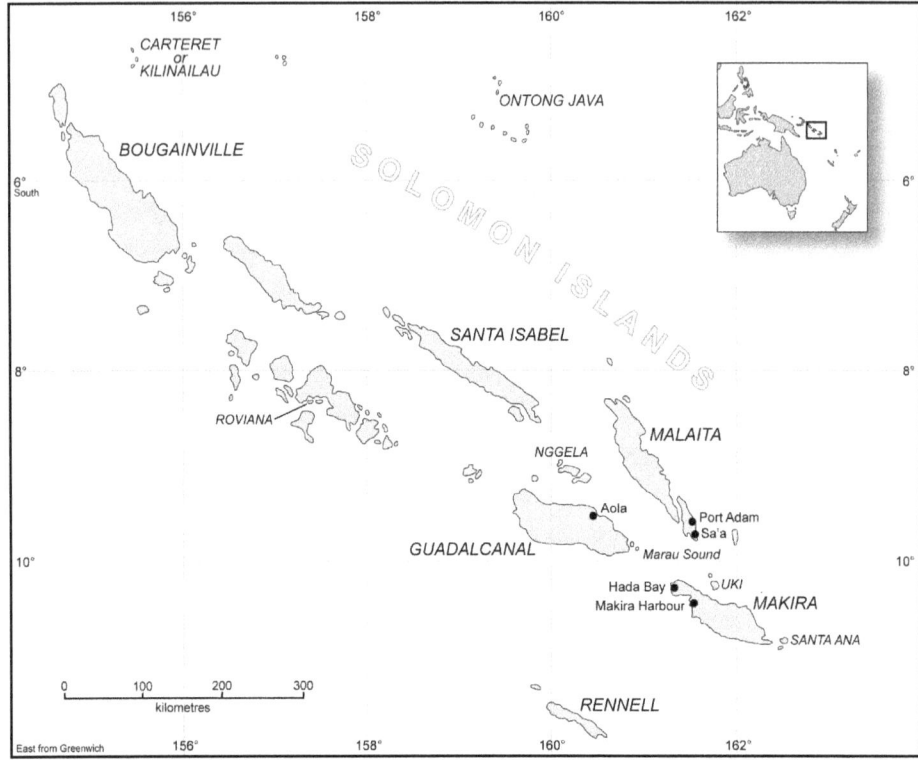

Figure 1. Map of Solomon Islands in 1885, showing the place names mentioned in the Crossan Diary.

Source: Author's map, drawn from the Crossan Diary and other sources.

Traces of traders

The men who came to the Western Pacific as traders were from diverse backgrounds and nationalities. Some were renegades from the law, a wife or other commitments. Driven by fear or social stigma, there were a few escaped convicts, as well as homosexuals, debtors and ne'er-do-wells. Many young men just sought adventure. Some were decent men who could not find sufficiently remunerative employment at home and hoped to make their fortunes. Several were well educated by the standards of the day.[8]

Well educated or not, few traders have left any personal records of their activities in the Solomon Islands. A few memoirs and sets of letters exist, along with a couple of rare diaries. As early as 1844, a bêche-de-mer and turtle

---

8 Bennett, *Wealth of the Solomons*, 58-60. Similar patterns existed elsewhere, see Munro, 'The lives and times of resident traders in Tuvalu: An exercise in history from below', *Pacific Studies* 10, 2 (March 1987): 79.

shell trader, Captain Andrew Cheyne in his memoirs talked of his brief but fraught business operations in the Solomons, mainly at Simbo, New Georgia and Sikaiana.[9] However, in the main Cheyne concentrated his operations and his recollections on Micronesia. In the 1860s Captain Alfred Tetens also left memoirs of his bêche de mer trading in Micronesia.[10] Neither Cheyne nor Tetens were truly resident traders although sometimes they employed such men as local agents, usually men who are only known to us via these two memoir writers. Nearer to the Solomon Islands, Frenchman Gustave Mouton wrote memoirs of his days in New Britain and New Ireland following the failure of the ill-fated Marquis du Rays's settlement of 1879-81. He managed to survive by trading and subsequently became a planter, a transition some Solomons traders also were to make. Mouton's memoirs were written well after the events and seem not to have been intended for publication.[11] One assumes these men either referred to ships' logs and diaries, or were just working from memory. Whatever, they often omitted day-to-day details in their memoirs.

Labour recruiters, such as William Wawn and 'Jock' Cromar, active in the Solomons and the rest of Melanesia, have left published books. Wawn had a brief stint as a copra trader in 1873 but had little to say about this activity as he soon took to recruiting. He was an educated and articulate apologist for the labour trade in an age when it was a target for Christian missionary and humanitarian concern. Using his logs, he recorded events that he witnessed relatively soon after they had occurred, with considerable detail and apparent accuracy, though he may well have 'tidied up' some of the less harmonious episodes.[12] Since shore-based traders could provide the goods that often were used to entice men to recruit, Wawn saw them as rivals. Cromar, writing over forty years after the events, is less concerned with the mundane routine of recruiting. He has much to say about dangerous encounters, including his own amorous interludes, with Melanesians from the New Hebrides across to New Guinea but is often vague about the timing of events. Although Cromar identified himself as a trader in the Marovo area of New Georgia his decades of life there subsequent to his inter-colonial recruiting experience are not recorded in the book. Almost all of what both Cromar and Wawn state briefly about traders concerns other men at work on shore, but tell us little about their lives in this role.[13] Similarly, missionaries,

---

9   Dorothy Shineberg, ed., *The trading voyages of Andrew Cheyne 1841-1844* (Canberra: Australian National University Press, 1971), 14, 303-313.
10 Alfred Tetens, *Among the Savages of the South Seas: Memoirs of Micronesia, 1862-1868*, trans. Florence Mann Spoehr, (Stanford: Stanford University Press, 1958).
11 Biskup, ed., *The New Guinea Memoirs*, 1-30.
12 Peter Corris, Editor's Introduction to William Wawn, *The South Sea Islanders and the Queensland Labour Trade: a Record of Voyages and Experiences in the Western Pacific, from 1875 to 1891* (Canberra: Australian National University Press, 1973), xxxii.
13 Wawn, *The South Sea Islanders*, 169, 199, 214, 217, 219-223, 246, 260, 286, 330-332, 344, 402; Cromar, *Jock of the Islands*, 77, 104, 112, 116, 133-135, 162-165, 166, 194-195, 255-257, 278.

commanders of warships and finally administrators such as Charles Woodford, the first Resident Commissioner of the Solomon Islands Protectorate, often provide brief observations of traders and their lives.[14]

More recently, selected letters (1875-1882) of Vernon Lee Walker, an Australian trader in the New Hebrides and New Caledonia along with some (1880-1882) by Louis Becke have been published.[15] In time, they are close to the period when William Crossan was trading in the islands. Most of their letters are addressed to their respective mothers. What one writes to one's mother is not always the same as what one might say to a peer and rarely what one would record in a diary. Above all, letters are couched to communicate between at least two people in some form of a relationship, to create or manage an impression, to convey the writer's image of her/himself as s/he wants the other to see, and so often excuse, explain, and thus both reveal and disguise.[16]

Not many traders in the Western Pacific wrote letters or kept diaries that have survived. Doug Munro points out, regarding the Ellice Islands (Tuvalu), that during the period c. 1860-1900 there were about seventy traders in total in the group, but only three have left letters or reminiscences - George Westbrook, Alfred Restieaux (mainly about other traders) and Louis Becke - and only one, George Winchcombe, has left a diary.[17]

Unlike the writers of memoirs and letters, there is little motive for the diarist to try to gloss daily events - unless, of course, he has plans for later publication for posterity. Even so, he knows he can excise or alter immediate reactions subsequently. There is nothing to indicate Crossan had a desire to write for anyone but himself. His diary is more memoranda than meditations, more commentary on commercial transactions than contemplations. At best, his prose is serviceable. Dull routine remains largely unadorned. Although brevity is Crossan's forte, the diary is also a kind of sympathetic if silent *socius*, a means through which he could express emotions and reactions that might have not been well received by Solomon Islanders or his sometime companions, Darrack and Griffiths. By today's standards his attitudes appear racist and his language is often 'politically incorrect', both being characteristics, along with his frustrations as a trader, which he shares with the letter-writers Walker and Becke. But in addition Crossan gives us glimpses of the humanity of the people he meets on Makira as well as showing his own empathy for their suffering and losses.

---

14 Bennett, *Wealth of the Solomons*, 419-424.
15 Nicholas Thomas and Richard Eves, eds, *Bad Colonists: The South Seas Letters of Vernon Lee Walker and Louis Becke* (Durham and London, Duke University Press, 1999).
16 Thomas and Eves, eds, *Bad Colonists*, 1-7.
17 Munro, 'The lives and times of resident traders', 99.

1. William Crossan

Early life

William Crossan, né Moffatt, was born in Victoria, Australia in December 1861, the son of William and Elizabeth Moffatt.[1] Moffatt senior came from Breage, Cornwall in about 1854, just as mining industries there began to decline. In January 1861 in Melbourne he married Elizabeth Deacon who was born in Roseneath, Tasmania where her father was a shoemaker.[2] In May 1862, at age 29, Moffatt died of injuries after he fell down a quartz mine shaft at the mining settlement of Whroo, near Bendigo (formerly Sandhurst) in Victoria (Figure 2). Young William, only five months old, never knew his father but carried the name Moffatt. His mother, aged 20 at the time of Moffatt's death, remarried eighteen months later. Her second husband was Thomas Crossan, a baker at Whroo, who at the time was 25 years of age. The eldest of twelve children, Thomas' parents came from Torphichen in Scotland where his father also had been a baker. Thomas seems to have migrated to Victoria in 1858 during the gold rushes and, according to the family historian, had with him his younger brother John and a sister called Agnes.[3]

Following the 1861 discovery of gold in Otago in New Zealand's South Island, Dunedin and nearby settlements were booming. The three siblings arrived in Dunedin in 1863, opened a bakery and general store at Milton and acquired land. The business prospered and Thomas Crossan's parents, John Snr and Agnes and the rest of his siblings migrated on the *Caribou* to New Zealand, joining their three children.[4] Certainly, by 1877, William Crossan and his wife Elizabeth had left Milton and were in business in Berwick. Said to have produced up to 4,000 loaves of bread a week,[5] they must have done well as the local 'draper, grocer, baker and every thing you can think of' since by 1881 they also had

---

[1] At this time names often had variant spelling; in this case, Moffit sometimes appears.
[2] Moffatt's parents were Benjamin and Elizabeth, née Gilbert. Entry 5298, Schedule of Deaths in the District of Rushworth, Bendigo Museum. Most of the Moffatt families of Breage were either copper or tin miners (1841 Census for the Parish of Breage in Cornwall, England available at http://freepages.genealogy.rootsweb.ancestry.com/~dtrounce/breagelists.html (Accessed 20 May 2009)). It is possible that an infant daughter was buried with Moffatt in Whroo as the gravestone mentions 'also Elizabeth' while it also states that stone was erected by 'his wife Elizabeth'(Headstone at Whroo Cemetery, May 1987 List, Bendigo Museum).
[3] Entry of marriage, No. 368, 2 Dec. 1863, St Andrews Bendigo, Bendigo Museum; G. S. Crossan, compiler, *A Baker's Dozen: A History of the Crossan Family and Descendants from 1792-1993* ([Dunedin, N.Z.? Privately printed]: G.S. Crossan, [1993]), 41; Thomas Crossan, ship *White Star*, Nov. 1858, Index to Unassisted Inward Passenger Lists for British, Foreign and New Zealand ports 1852-1923, Public Records Office Victoria. Oddly, only Thomas is listed as on board the *White Star*, with no mention of John Jnr and Agnes Jnr.
[4] Thomas and Elizabeth sold out the bakery business in Milton and bought a local hotel, the Criterion in about 1876. John Jnr and Agnes Jnr had moved to Roxburgh where their parents settled (Crossan, *A Baker's Dozen*, 4, 30). The author does not mention that William was the son of William Moffat.
[5] Crossan, *A Baker's Dozen*, 41.

property at Tokomairiro leased to a former employee.⁶ Thomas and Elizabeth had seven children, besides William – Jack (John Robert), Richard, Agnes, Elizabeth, Margaret, Mary and Isabel Jane.⁷ When William was about nineteen, presumably because of his experience in the store of his parents, he obtained a position with Robert Scobie in the nearby town of Clinton (Figure 3).

Figure 2. The grave of William Moffatt, father of William Crossan, in Whroo, Victoria, Australia. The headstone reads: 'Erected by Elizabeth in memory of her beloved Husband William Moffatt, Native of Cornwall, England, who lost his life by falling down the shaft of the Albert Claim at Whroo on the 22nd May 1862 aged 29 years. A Husband kind and a Father dear, a faithful friend he lieth here.'

Source: Photograph taken by Anne Forden and Janey Jackson, February 2011.

---

6 William Crossan, Copy of letter to an Aunt in Victoria, 1881, in William Crossan, Misc-MS-1224, Hocken Library (see Appendix 1).
7 *Otago Witness*, 23 Oct. 1901, 43, 4 Apr. 1906, 65, 12 Jun. 1901, 43. Isabel Jane died aged 19 in October 1901. In his letter to his aunt in Australia, William refers to his grandfather and uncles, which indicates that other members of his parents' families also had migrated to the district. There were several people with the name of Crossan in the region at this time (see Appendix 1).

Figure 3. Portrait found within the William Crossan diary-notebook, and presumed to depict the author. The date is unknown, but it could be the same photograph that Crossan mentions in the draft letter to his Australian aunt written in 1881 (Appendix 1), where he states 'I got my Photo taken to send you over but I have left them at home'.

Crossan as Otago storeman

In about October of 1881, two months before his twentieth birthday, William wrote about his new job in a letter he drafted to his aunt in Australia:

> I am Head Storman for Robert Scobie a large Storkeeper up here [in Clinton]. I thought in my mind I would take a short trip from home for a shortish time to see what the world is like and I am getting on fine. It is the first situation ever I was at in my life but I am pretty well up in the Storekeeping Business. I am going to make it my profession.[8]

---

[8] William Crossan, in William Crossan Diary, Misc-MS-1224, Hocken Library (see Appendix 1).

With this, Crossan began keeping a notebook cum diary and accounts book. On subsequent pages of his notebook he demonstrates some progress in fulfilling this ambition as storekeeper, but also some setbacks. His boss Robert Scobie was a man of some standing in the community. A member of the regional Clutha council and a donor of prizes at the Clinton Ploughing Match, he had been made a Justice of the Peace in 1879.[9] A little before November 1881, Scobie had taken out insurance on two separate lots of oats owned by the brothers Haugh over which he had a lien on a debt. Mysteriously, the oats were destroyed by fire in two separate incidents, which occasioned a court inquiry. William Crossan was a major witness at the hearing as he was in the employ of Scobie. But his testimony in early February 1882 was somewhat equivocal and differed from an earlier statement he had made to police re the loss by fire of the oats. In what appeared an insurance scam, perhaps perpetrated with the connivance of the Haugh brothers and/or Scobie, the jury found the fire to be caused by person or persons unknown.[10] Crossan had been clearly upset by the prospect of a court case as he rehearsed his answers to likely questions in his notebook.[11]

Crossan's brief and scribbled diary entries of this period of his life begin on 20th February 1882 and continue intermittently until 10th May of that year. He was still employed as Scobie's storekeeper in Clinton, but some tensions in the relationship are apparent. On Friday 28th March, after packing up butter for Dunedin, Crossan records that he 'helped to sort horses then went down the town, played a few games of billiards', before returning to his lodgings 'exactly at midnight'. His employer Scobie came into his room and accused him of coming home late the night before ('it was a falsehood'), and the following day his boss was 'very sulky and would not speak'. Crossan confides to his diary on Sunday 30th April, 'Raining incessantly all day. Will be very glad when this time next month turns up and then off I go no more slavery'.[12] His first step towards achieving this aim was to move from Otago to Auckland.

Auckland and the Islands trade

William Crossan left Scobie's employ in about May 1882. The following year he was in Auckland but remained in touch with his stepfather. In the notebook are accounts that show Thomas Crossan of Berwick loaning William £110.00 in 1883. William repaid £40.00 by means of two cash transactions, but his

---

9 *Otago Witness*, 13 Jan. 1877, 10, 10 Aug. 1878, 3, 14 Sep. 1878, 7, 29 Mar. 1879.
10 *Otago Witness*, 11 Feb. 1882, 11, *Tuapeka Times*, 18 Mar. 1889, 3.
11 William Crossan, Diary, Hocken Library, Dunedin. Scobie did not lose by the fires, but in 1888 not only did he suffer the death of his 15-year-old son, he also became bankrupt and left the district to try his luck on a sheep run in the Te Anau district, which is where he died in 1900. *Otago Witness*, 27 July 1888, 21, 17 Aug. 1888, 19, 26 Oct. 1899, 43; 5 Dec. 1900, 33.
12 William Crossan, Diary, Hocken Library, intermittent diary entries for Feb.-Apr. 1882.

indebtedness to his stepfather increased in July 1883 after Thomas had sent him further payments in cash, by cheque, and in kind – 165 lbs butter and 9 firkins of butter. Following these various transactions, when Crossan again calculated the balance (probably in 1884) the total loan stood at £111.17.0 which represented about nine month's salary for a storeman. Running into debt may have been inevitable at this time of economic recession, but even so Crossan's position must have been humiliating for someone with his strict moral code.[13] Possibly it was one reason for William Crossan's decision to enter into the risky but potentially lucrative Fiji and Solomons trade.

As well as the debt that he owed to his stepfather, there may have been other reasons for William Crossan's restlessness and desire to travel. Perhaps when he was young he felt he was a little outside the Crossan family, as he was not legally adopted and later registered his marriage in the name of Moffat. Yet he was known as Crossan, spoke respectfully of his step-father Thomas, and it seems that William's descendants and probably his siblings were never aware that his biological father was William Moffatt.[14] Moreover, when his mother Elizabeth died in 1923, aged 81, at her son's hotel, William Crossan's age was stated as 60, making his year of birth 1863, the same year as her marriage to Thomas. Since William was likely to have been on the scene and knew his own birth date to be December 1861, it is strange that this anomaly found its way into the record.[15] Perhaps by then he felt confident enough to represent himself as really a Crossan.

In the 1880s, however, wider forces were at work and may have given Crossan added impetus to seek his fortune elsewhere. By 1880, the South Island of New Zealand was in economic depression, with the most southerly provinces of Otago and Southland the worst affected. The gold was almost mined out, the Australian colonies were no longer paying high prices for wheat, and the banks reduced credit and increased interest on loans. Bankruptcies were increasing while the land was suffering from massive rabbit infestations and consequent loss of pasture on land often already over-stocked. The depression had spread to the North Island by 1885, just as Julius Vogel returned to the national parliament. One of Vogel's enduring dreams since he was Premier in the 1870s had been to make New Zealand the hub of trade and commerce with the South Pacific and in due course to persuade Britain to make the region a British lake. In so doing, the defence of New Zealand from the rest of the great powers would be guaranteed. All this talk in the parliament and in newspapers could inspire similar visions for a profitable trading career for a young man in the Pacific Islands.[16]

---

13   Crossan, in William Crossan Diary, Misc-MS-1224, Hocken Library (see Appendix 2, 'All goods at the time of arrival...').
14   Crossan, *A Baker's Dozen*.
15   Entry for Elizabeth Crossan, District of Dunedin, Registration no. 1923/9651, Register of Births, Deaths and Marriages, New Zealand.
16   Angus Ross, *New Zealand's Aspirations in the Pacific in the Nineteenth Century* (Oxford: Clarendon Press, 1964), 106-130, 157-172; Erik Olssen and Marcia Stenson, *A Century of Change: New Zealand 1800-1900* (Auckland: Longman Paul, 1990), 284-289.

For New Zealand, Auckland was the centre for commercial firms with interests in the Pacific islands. In 1884 William Crossan was working there as a storeman for an import and export business, probably McArthur and Co., provisioning ships on the Pacific run and serving customers and merchants in Sydney, Mago Island in Fiji, and Apia in Samoa. The company also imported tropical products such as fruit, coconuts, and coral. It was thus that he learned the exchange value of tobacco for copra and onions for yams.[17] Copra was used in making candles and soap, much of it being purchased by the Union Oil, Soap and Candle Company factory opened in 1883 at Mount Richmond, Auckland.[18] By the mid-1880s a great deal of island copra went to Auckland with ships usually taking cargo to Fiji and from there or from other islands getting a backloading of copra.[19] It is likely that at this time he met a man called Darrack who was to go with him to the Solomon Islands as a boatbuilder. The Darrack family were in that business in north Auckland.[20]

At this point, Crossan almost certainly worked in Samoa for McArthur and Co. and visited Fiji, which is perhaps where he met a man called Baker who was active in the Solomons trade. It was from Suva, the new capital of the British colony of Fiji, that Crossan, Darrack, and Baker sailed along with able seaman Edward (Ned) Griffiths to Solomon Islands on the labour ship *Glencairn*, arriving in Hada Bay in the Arosi language region of north west Makira, in late August 1885. Crossan thus began his life as a copra trader. Six months later on 4th March 1886, with Baker and Darrack already gone, Crossan and Griffiths left on the *Glencairn* bound for Auckland.

His later life

After Crossan returned to Auckland he went on to Otago and probably worked as a baker in the Dunstan area.[21] In 1889 he is recorded as back in his home at Berwick, engaged mainly in storekeeping as well as running stock, mining, training and breeding race horses, and carrying out earth works.[22] His stepfather, Thomas died in October 1894 and William remained with his mother assisting in the store at Berwick.[23] He and his mother, Elizabeth, are mentioned

---

17   Crossan, Diary, accounting entries for August-October 1884.
18   *Observer*, 15 Aug. 1908, 26; Ellerslie Heritage. http://www.ellerslie.net.nz/heritage/businesses.asp (Accessed 29 May 2009). Much copra was similarly processed at Lever Brothers' Balmain factory in Sydney.
19   See for example Statement of Q. M. Anderson, mate of *Kate McGregor*, 6 July 1885, Colonial Office 225/18 (West Pacific 15521), The National Archives, Kew.
20   *Daily Southern Cross*, 30 Sep. 1875, 2.
21   New Zealand Electoral Rolls 1885/86, 1890, 1886. http://www.ancestry.com/ (Accessed 23 March 2011).
22   *Tuapeka Times*, 4 Jul. 1885, 3, 3 Dec. 1892, 3, 4 Dec. 1895, 6, 5 Feb. 1896, 2, 8. Feb. 1896, 4, 5 Aug. 1899, 3, 11 Nov. 1899, 2, 31 Jan. 1900, 2, 4 Apr. 1900, 3, 2 May 1900, 3, 5 Dec. 1900, 3; *Otago Witness*, 10 Mar. 1892, 27, 23 Aug. 1894, 26, 6 Oct. 1898, 28, 16 Aug. 1900, 39, 29 May 1901, 32, 30 Jul. 1902, 24.
23   *Otago Witness*, 18 Oct. 1894, 27, 28 July 1898, 27.

in the court proceedings on at least four occasions. They appeared twice as creditors of local bankrupts,[24] and twice because of alleged selling of 'sly grog' at the Berwick sheep dog trials and at the store respectively; however, the evidence against them from their loyal customers was that 'no money passed' so the charges were dismissed.[25] Elizabeth was well known in the community not only as storekeeper but also the caterer at most social events.[26] The 'sly grog' charges apparently did not harm William's reputation among the rural community and the fact that his house was designated the local polling booth in the national election in 1890 indicates he was a trusted citizen.[27]

In March 1906 the local citizens at Berwick gave William Crossan a large farewell and presented with 'a well-filled purse of sovereigns' on the 'approach of his marriage.' At age 45 he married Ellen (Nellie) Hall, 22 years of age, of Tuapeka, on 28th March 1906 at Outram and settled in Dunedin where he became the proprietor of the Waterloo Hotel, Ruskin Street in the suburb of Caversham.[28] Except for another court appearance for selling sly grog through the post in 1915 he seems to have faded from the public record and was retired by 1925.[29] He died in September 1936, aged 74 and his wife, Ellen died in March 1948, aged 63.[30] Two children were born of the marriage, Gladys and William.[31] Perhaps they too have left a trace of their existence in this diary-notebook. It contains child-like printing on odd pages including a part of a nursery rhyme. And on a loose scrap of paper a recipe for 'hair restorer' has been jotted down, both clues to the passing of the years in Crossan's life. The last historical record that refers to William Crossan is from 1987 when his long lost diary-notebook was presented to the Hocken Library in Dunedin, 'found in an old desk' by a Dunedin clergyman of the Church of England, the same denomination that had laboured to bring Christianity to the Arosi people of Makira where Crossan had once been a trader.[32]

---

24 *Tuapeka Times*, 6 Feb. 1897, 3, *Otago Witness*, 9 Nov. 1904, 14.
25 *Timaru Herald*, 25 Jul. 1898, 3, *Otago Witness*, 28 July 1898, 27, 22 Sept. 1898, 20.
26 *Otago Witness*, 31 Jul. 1907, 73.
27 *Tuapeka Times*, 6 Dec. 1899, 4.
28 William signed the register as William Moffatt, so it seems unlikely Thomas Crossan ever legally adopted him (Entry 1906/3745 (Marriages), Register of Births, Deaths and Marriages, New Zealand; Marriage Register, Church of England, West Taieri, entry for 28 March 1906, Hocken Library; Entry for William Crossan, http://www.dunedin.govt.nz/facilities/cemeteries/cemeteries_search?recordid=12504&type=Burial (Accessed 23 April 2009)).
29 *Evening Post*, 7 Sep. 1915, 3. They resided at 3 Sussex Street, South Dunedin. His mother Elizabeth died in 1923 (Electoral rolls, 1911-1931 http://caversham.otago.ac.nz/electors/erid.php?erkey=15215 (Accessed 20 May 2009)).
30 Site 1455, Block 136, Plot 46, Anderson's Bay Cemetery, Headstone Transcriptions, bound typescript, Vol. 4. Hocken Library.
31 Crossan, *A Baker's Dozen*, 43.
32 Hocken Library, Dunedin, New Zealand: Accession Register, note on William Crossan ms, 1987, Misc-MS-1224.

2. Makira islanders and Europeans

Makira and European contact

William Crossan wrote his Solomon Islands diary while he was a resident for six months at Hada Bay. Hada is at the western end of the island then known as San Cristoval but today usually called Makira Island, in the south-east Solomons (Figure 1). The people living in this part of Makira now number about 7,000 and they speak the Arosi language, which gives its name to the whole district. Charles Fox, the Anglican missionary who lived at Pamua on the north coast from 1911-1924, described the area as follows:

> Arosi is not a very large district – about sixty miles of coastline with about thirty villages, and now only a few villages inland, most of the latter very small. ... This western end of the island is largely limestone, ... but the interior of the limestone country consists of a high and breezy plateau with very deep and steep intersecting valleys, sometimes as steep as a Colorado canyon, so that two villages almost inaccessible by path are within hail of each other.[1]

Crossan's trading activities only involved the coastal villages. Those that he visited in 1885-86 are shown in Figure 4.

There had been sporadic contact between whaling ships and the people of San Cristoval or Makira Island since the first such record in 1799. By the late 1840s Makira Harbour in the south was well known to whalers and traders as a secure anchorage with easy access to wood and water, pigs, fruit, vegetables and women.[2] Curios, shells and turtle shell could also be bartered, and on average about three whaling ships a year came to the harbour in the period 1850-70.[3] For a while Makira Harbour was the headquarters of the ill-fated Catholic Marist Mission, which operated there from 1845 to 1847 before withdrawing.[4]

In the North West season (November to April) Hada Bay was much less sheltered than Makira Harbour, but it too became known as a relatively safe haven for visiting ships. Along with Makira Harbour, Hada was one of the few places in Solomon Islands with its own Admiralty chart, based on surveys by H.M.S. *Cordelia* in 1861. The chart shows an anchorage with depths of 7-23 fathoms. At

---

1   Charles E. Fox, *The Threshold of the Pacific: An Account of the Social Organisation, Magic and Religion of the People of San Cristoval in the Solomon Islands* (London: Kegan Paul, Trench, Trubner, 1924), 7-8.
2   David Hilliard, *God's Gentlemen: A History of the Melanesian Mission, 1849-1902* (St Lucia, Queensland: University of Queensland Press, 1978), 82-83; Bennett, *Wealth of the Solomons*, 27.
3   Bennett, *Wealth of the Solomons*, 29.
4   Hugh Laracy, *Marists and Melanesians: A History of Catholic Missions in the Solomon Islands*. (Canberra: Australian National University Press, 1976), 20-22.

the head of the bay there is a river mouth ('good water, small boats can enter HW [at High Water]'). The bay is flanked north and south by cliffs, and in the middle there is a 'steep gravel beach' backing on to 'low brush wood'.[5] Perhaps the earliest depiction of Hada Bay was by Cecil Foljambe, who sketched the view from H.M.S. *Curaçoa* when it anchored there for three days in September 1865 (Figure 5).

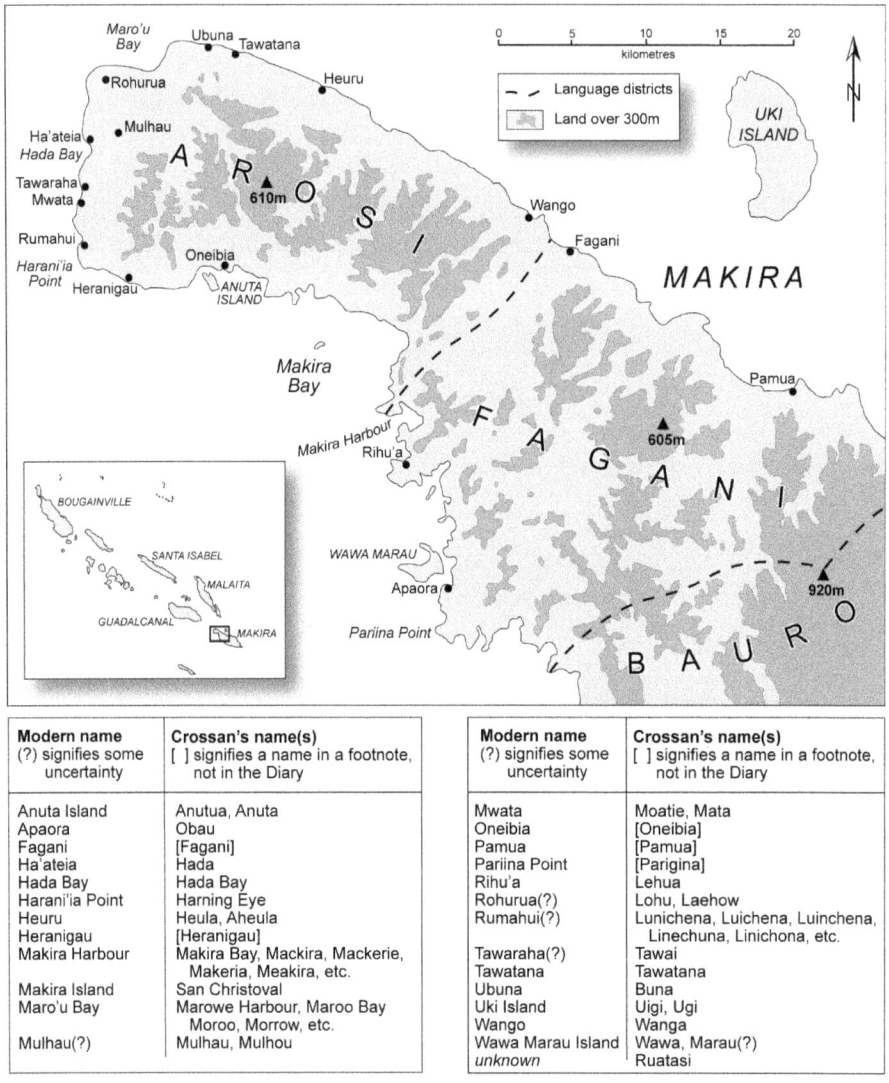

Modern name (?) signifies some uncertainty	Crossan's name(s) [ ] signifies a name in a footnote, not in the Diary
Anuta Island	Anutua, Anuta
Apaora	Obau
Fagani	[Fagani]
Ha'ateia	Hada
Hada Bay	Hada Bay
Harani'ia Point	Harning Eye
Heuru	Heula, Aheula
Heranigau	[Heranigau]
Makira Harbour	Makira Bay, Mackira, Mackerie, Makeria, Meakira, etc.
Makira Island	San Christoval
Maro'u Bay	Marowe Harbour, Maroo Bay, Moroo, Morrow, etc.
Mulhau(?)	Mulhau, Mulhou

Modern name (?) signifies some uncertainty	Crossan's name(s) [ ] signifies a name in a footnote, not in the Diary
Mwata	Moatie, Mata
Oneibia	[Oneibia]
Pamua	[Pamua]
Pariina Point	[Parigina]
Rihu'a	Lehua
Rohurua(?)	Lohu, Laehow
Rumahui(?)	Lunichena, Luichena, Luinchena, Linechuna, Linichona, etc.
Tawaraha(?)	Tawai
Tawatana	Tawatana
Ubuna	Buna
Uki Island	Uigi, Ugi
Wango	Wanga
Wawa Marau Island	Wawa, Marau(?)
unknown	Ruatasi

Figure 4. Map of Arosi district and adjacent parts of Makira Island, showing language boundaries and the place names mentioned in the Crossan Diary.

Source: Author's map, drawn from the Crossan Diary and other sources.

---

5   Admiralty, Plan 209, *South West Pacific, Anchorages in the Solomon Islands*. London: British Admiralty, 1864.

Figure 5. Hada Bay in 1865 as depicted by Cecil Foljambe (1868: 206).

Source: Early New Zealand Books, University of Auckland Library <http://www.enzb.auckland.ac.nz/document?wid=2224&p=1>

Julius Brenchley was also on H.M.S. *Curaçoa* and he described Hada Bay as follows:

> The bay, though very small, is snug and safe; the high cliff on either side is picturesque, and densely covered with wood, and at the bottom of there is a flat, well-wooded beach backed by lofty hills... The village [lay] one or two miles distant at the point of the bay.[6]

Brenchley was told that it might be unwise to go to the village, today's Ha'ateia, and he decided to stay near the beach. Possibly in 1865 Ha'ateia was located just inland from the coast, and certainly no coastal village is shown on the 1861 Admiralty chart. Foljambe believed that Hada Bay lacked any coastal settlement:

> Recherche [Hada] Bay... There is no village here, the settlement is in the next bay to the southward. I walked round a point on the right, and after a walk of four miles came to the village [Tawaraha]. We shot some pigeons on the way there. I found the Bishop [Patteson] there, and as he

---

6   Julius L. Brenchley, *Jottings during the Cruise of H.M.S. Curaçoa among the Islands of the South Seas* (London: Longman, Green & Co, 1873), 270, 272.

had come by boat, he was quite surprised to see us arrive on foot. I got a few little curiosities here, such as bracelets, ear-rings, &c, and walked back in the afternoon by the beach...[7]

Despite there being 'no village here', on the second day of *Curaçoa*'s visit there were crowds of people in Hada Bay engaged in barter trade on the beach and paddling out to the ship in their canoes, bringing spears, clubs, parrots, opossums, pigs, fowls, yams and taro, to exchange for tobacco, beads, pipes, fish hooks and other things. The visitors on *Curaçoa* found that, unlike on Ulawa and Uki where hoop iron was still in demand, in Hada Bay 'nothing was taken here more greedily than stick tobacco; one could get almost anything for a small piece, even more than for a tomahawk'.[8] It would appear that previous bartering with whalers and traders had reduced local demand for iron, but it was replaced by an insatiable demand for the new narcotic.

In political terms, too, it is apparent that in 1865 the people in Hada Bay were already well accustomed to receiving visiting ships. H.M.S. *Curaçoa* had steamed into the bay during a flat calm, towing the Melanesian Mission sailing ship *Southern Cross*, and both ships anchored. Almost at once, Brenchley reported, 'a native, calling himself the King, an oldish looking fellow, came on board and showed the commodore some certificates', and later that day he presented the commodore with a pig and other gifts. This unnamed Hada Bay big-man or chief was clearly knowledgeable in the white man's ways, even though one of his 'certificates' described him as 'a bore' and another warned that 'he was an old knave and the less you have to do with him the better'.[9] This was probably the same man who was named in 1877 as 'King Ledger'.[10]

In addition to the King coming on board H.M.S. *Curaçoa* 'another native came also who spoke English'.[11] This interpreter might have been a returned labourer from Queensland, or perhaps someone who had worked on ships, like the old man on the beach who addressed Brenchley 'using coarse Hawaiian gibberish, no doubt derived from traders'.[12] Alternatively the English-speaking interpreter might have been a young Sono, who later was himself described as the Hada Bay chief. Twenty years later it was Sono, under the name Johnstone, who acted as go-between with the New Zealanders when Baker and Crossan came to Hada Bay to trade for copra.

---

7   C. Foljambe, *Three Years on the Australia Station* (187 Piccadilly, London: Hatchard & Co., for private circulation, 1868), 206-7.
8   Foljambe, *Three Years*, 206.
9   Brenchley, *Jottings*, 270.
10 Cairns correspondent, The voyage of the Loelia, *Australian Town and Country Journal*, 3 November 1877, 17.
11 Brenchley, *Jottings*, 270.
12 Brenchley, *Jottings*, 272.

Hada Bay as a trading station

It is clear that when William Crossan records his landing from the schooner *Glencairn* at Hada Bay in early September 1885, he was entering a Melanesian world that was already in a state of transition. By the 1880s foreigners, their practices and their technologies were familiar to many coastal people in Arosi district, although the bush people were still largely uncontacted by the outside world, except perhaps for a few who managed to pass safely to the coast. The people on the western Arosi coast had looked after castaways and deserters from 1851 onwards.[13] Living at Hada Bay in 1865 were two American survivors from a whaling ship wrecked on Indispensable Reef, one black man and one white man.[14] By the 1870s 'blackbirders' (labour recruiting ships) were also regular visitors. The *Isabella* managed to recruit three interpreters in Hada Bay for its recruiting voyage to Guadalcanal, Malaita and then back to Makira, in 1871.[15] The *Woodlark* spent two weeks in the bay in August 1871 making repairs and trying to secure the services of an interpreter, and during this period two other Queensland ships arrived. The Government Agent on board *Woodlark* wrote as follows:

> There are no known harbours to the westward of Hadda Bay, where repairs could be executed, and as our foreyard was unsound, rotten, it was a matter of vital importance to reach some secure port in order to replace the worthless spar with a fresh one. Hadda Bay is ... sheltered from the prevalent winds (south-east trades), but fully exposed to westerly winds .... There are no islanders residing here, but many come from the settlements along the coast, bringing native products for barter. They appear friendly and obliging, and a white man who has been left here as security for the return of a native accompanying a Fijian schooner through the group, speaks well of their kindness and hospitality.[16]

Less fortunate was the schooner *Lytonna*, labour recruiter from Brisbane, which struck a reef and was wrecked in Hada Bay during a storm in November 1875. All the recruits on board got ashore, however, and 'during the stay on the island the shipwrecked people being well armed, did not suffer any inconvenience from the natives, who supplied them with yams and other necessary articles.'[17]

Missionaries on Makira seem to have experienced greater difficulties. The Marist Mission had failed to get established in Makira Bay in 1847 and it was

---

13 Bennett, *Wealth of the Solomons*, 29-30, 356, 378.
14 O. Rietmann, *Wanderungen in Australien und Polynesien* (St Gallen: Scheitlin & Zollikofer, 1868),183-4.
15 *The Brisbane Courier*, Cruise of the Isabella to the Polynesian Islands, 8 November 1871, 3.
16 Recruiting Polynesians, *The Brisbane Courier*, 14 December 1871, 3.
17 Wreck of the Lyttona, *The Queenslander* (Brisbane), 18 December 1875, 8.

not until 1870 that Christian missionaries returned. In that year the Melanesian Mission (Church of England) founded its first school on the island at Wango on Arosi's north coast. The first missionaries at Wango were the Englishman Joseph Atkin and Stephen Taroaniara from nearby Tawatana village, both of whom were killed the following year at Nukapu in the Reef Islands alongside Bishop Patteson. In 1872 another Englishman Robert Jackson arrived at Wango and the school was revived, but Jackson had little success and he left in 1874. According to the Rev. C.H. Brooke,

> [A] visit to Wango is not encouraging; the few people who remain have already received an untoward bias [against Europeans] from the constant succession of vessels – traders, whalers and slavers – which have made the beautiful bay their habitual resort.[18]

Another Melanesian Mission school was started further east at Fagani, and then a third in 1882 at Heuru, but the number of Christian converts remained very small.[19]

Figure 6. Photograph of a man spearing fish and fishing stands at Heuru, 1906. The steam ship in the background is probably the Anglican mission ship, *Southern Cross*. The same picture is reproduced by Rannie (1912: 293) with the following caption: 'San Christoval Islands. Fishing scaffolds on the outer reef. The man in the foreground is fishing with a four-pronged spear. In this way he catches mullet, bream, cod-fish, rays and small sharks. (J.W. Beattie, Hobart)'.

Source: Bishop Terry Brown, Honiara, from J. W. Beattie photographic collection, 1906.

---

18   C. H. Brooke, 'Progress of the Melanesian Mission'. *Mission Life* 4: 1873, 442. http://anglicanhistory.org/oceania/brooke_progress1873.html (Accessed January 2011).
19   Charles E. Fox, *Lord of the Southern Isles, being the Story of the Anglican Mission in Melanesia 1849-1949* (London: A.R. Mowbray, 1958), 160.

2. Makira islanders and Europeans

Figure 7. Photograph of David Boo, 1906. A younger man in 1886, Boo was the chief of Heuru.

Source: Bishop Terry Brown, Honiara, from J. W. Beattie photographic collection, 1906.

Figure 8. The beach at Heuru, north coast of Arosi District, 1906. Twenty years earlier Heuru village was the furthest place that Crossan reached in his sailing cutter, trading for copra.

Source: Bishop Terry Brown, Honiara, from J. W. Beattie photographic collection, 1906.

A trading station had already existed at Hada some years beforehand, but when Baker and Crossan arrived in 1885 there is no mention that other foreigners were present. The Hada trading station was probably initiated in 1877 by G. Atkinson acting for McArthur & Co., a New Zealand trading firm, the likely Auckland employer of Crossan in 1884. In March 1877, the company sent the *Mary Anderson* to install about seventeen agents on commission in the Solomon Islands, and a number of these were located on the north side of Makira. Others were also showing an interest in this relatively hospitable coastline. In about July 1877 a labour recruiting vessel arrived off Hada Bay:

> Off Recherche [Hada] Bay, a chief came out in his canoe and informed them [the ship *Loelia*] that the *May Douglas*, brigantine, Captain Brown, was lying inside. She is engaged in the island trade, and was looking for a place to form a station, having not done so at that time, but intended to proceed further north.[20]

---

20 Cairns correspondent, The voyage of the Loelia, *Australian Town and Country Journal*, 3 November 1877, 17.

The *Glencairn* — a typical Schooner

Figure 9. The schooner *Glencairn*, 62 tons, was built of kauri in Auckland in the early 1880s and soon went into the islands' trade. This labour recruiting ship took William Crossan to and from Makira. In September 1900, she was wrecked when carrying timbers on the east coast of New Zealand. She ran into a storm before reaching the port of Timaru and turned north, back to Akaroa but sank off Ninety Mile Beach (*Timaru Herald*, 2 October 1900, 4).

Source: Hocken Collections, Uare Taoka o Hakena, University of Otago, Dunedin with permission of the Timaru Port Authority from C. E. Hassall (compiler), *A Short History of the Port of Timaru*, Timaru: Timaru Harbour Board, 1955, 94.

The following year it was reported that at Hada Bay 'a white man was left here by the *Douglas* to collect copra'.[21] The McArthur company decided to withdraw from the Solomon Islands in 1878 after one of their traders, Townsend, was killed and his companion, a white boy, was speared at Uki.[22] In 1879 the trader at Hada was James Martin, working as agent for Captain Brodie (*Ariel*), but Martin soon left Hada for Wango.[23]

---

21 The cruise of the Isabella, *Morning Bulletin* (Rockhampton, Queensland), 2 August 1878, 2.
22 Entry 22 May, 1877, Journal of Mr Charles Hunter on Southern Cross, 1877, http://anglicanhistory.org/oceania/brown1877/ (Accessed December 2011); *Auckland Star*, 30 September 1878, 2.
23 Bennett, *Wealth of the Solomons*, 377.

There is no further evidence of a station at Hada Bay until 1885, suggesting a gap in trading activity and perhaps explaining the eagerness of chief Sono (Johnstone) to assist the New Zealanders when they arrived there. The next record concerns 'Baker, Crossan & Co of Fiji' and refers to Crossan's arrival at Hada on 28th August 1885.[24] No formal record of this company can be found, and it is likely to have been an entirely informal arrangement among the partners. Baker with Darrack (whose given names are never mentioned) and Crossan travelled from Suva on the schooner *Glencairn*, which was engaged in returning labourers from Fiji (Figure 9).[25]

According to the man overseeing labour transactions, the Government Agent on board, the newcomers who were off shore from Hada on 28th August 'intended to establish their trading station there'. Next day, Baker purchased 'a piece of land' and arranged to have a house built, and the three men went ashore. Some of the returning labourers who were aboard also came ashore for some exercise and a wash, and some of these men worked for the day with Darrack building the house and in return were paid with pipes and tobacco.[26] Darrack stayed behind at Hada to superintend the building of a sailing cutter to be used in Crossan's copra trading.

After leaving Hada Bay on 3rd September, the ship *Glencairn* continued its voyage around the Solomon Islands including Malaita, the major source of indentured labour. With all returnees landed, the ship returned to Hada on 19th October to collect Crossan's copra, stock up on firewood and water, and add ballast to the virtually empty vessel.[27] Darrack, his work finished, also came on board. He had spent the previous two months working with Crossan and Johnstone (known as Johnson as well as Sono), the big man or chief of Hada, building the sailing cutter that was to prove crucial for the success of Crossan's trading network. Later, Johnstone was able to use this boat himself for travelling around the coasts of Arosi district. Baker as well as Darrack went back to Suva on the *Glencairn*, arriving 12th December with three tons of copra from Crossan's and Baker's operations.[28]

Meanwhile, able seaman Ned Griffiths had decided to work as a 'hut keeper' for Crossan and left the *Glencairn* on 31st October 1885 before it sailed for Suva.[29] Griffiths remained at Hada Bay with Crossan until 4th March 1886. In late February 1886, however, Griffiths, 'without any sufficient provocation', had shot

---

24 Bennett, *Wealth of the Solomons*, 378.
25 G. Pilkington, Journal of *Glencairn*, 1 August-8 December 1885, Government Agents' Logbooks No. 56, National Archives of Fiji (NAF), Suva.
26 G. Pilkington, Journal of *Glencairn*, No. 56, 1 August-8 December 1885, No. 56, NAF.
27 G. Pilkington, Journal of *Glencairn*, Aug.-Dec. 1885, No. 56, NAF.
28 *Suva Times*, 12 Dec. 1885, NAF, Suva. This reference was kindly provided by Prof. Ian Campbell.
29 *Fiji Times*, 1 Aug. 1885; G. Pilkington, Journal of *Glencairn*, Aug.-Dec. 1885, No. 56, NAF.

a local man through the cheek.[30] At this time, if Crossan's sketchy comments are any indication, Ned Griffiths was suffering from recurrent bouts of fever, almost certainly malaria. Such illness could have clouded his judgement and frayed his temper. Crossan would undoubtedly have been shocked by this incident and anxious about its consequences. It is perhaps for this reason that he makes no mention of it in his diary, realising the significance of such a document if there were to be a murder enquiry. He must also have been extremely nervous about the possibility of retaliation towards the white men at Hada Bay, though at the time Johnstone's intervention had protected Griffiths.[31] As Crossan noted in his diary entry for 11th January 1886,

> The Bushmen have just killed one Boy belonging to Chief of Lunichena, a return just back from Port McKay. So much for civilized San Christoval [Makira], this is no. 4 that has got his quick dispatch, with one white man, in 4 months, that I know of.

It was perhaps to avoid a similar fate that Crossan and Griffiths decided to leave Makira as soon as possible. Perhaps too Griffiths' repeated bouts of malaria necessitated removal from the Solomon Islands. Even though the man he had injured was said to be 'quite recovered',[32] a few days later their opportunity came when the *Glencairn* arrived from Fiji on another voyage to return recruits. On 4th March, after collecting copra at Makira Harbour, Crossan and Griffiths left Hada on the *Glencairn* for Auckland, which offered a market for the copra and a safe homecoming for William Crossan.

There is no record of the total tonnage of all the copra Crossan produced and sold, but he was operating in a period of falling prices. From as high as £32 a ton on the London market, copra fluctuated in price around £20 in the early 1880s and began to fall to a level below £15 per ton in 1886, not to recover until 1901. Crossan's profit on each ton was probably much the same as other Solomon traders, around £2.5 to £3, after recompensing his Solomon agents and shipping costs, but this excludes payments to other Westerners involved at various stages, such as Darrack, Baker and Griffiths.[33] Life as a Solomons trader did not pay well in terms of the risks involved. Perhaps this explains why Crossan abandoned his Pacific Islands ambitions. He put away his Solomon Islands diary-notebook, and seems never to have used it again.

---

30 G. Pilkington, Journal of *Glencairn*, Dec. 1885-Mar. 1886, Government Agents' Logbooks, No. 58, NAF.
31 Acting Agent of Immigration to Secretary of High Commission, 18 May 1886, Western Pacific High Commission (hereafter WPHC) 79/86, Western Pacific Archives (hereafter WPA), University of Auckland, Auckland.
32 G. Pilkington, Journal of *Glencairn*, Dec. 1885-Mar. 1886, No. 58, NAF.
33 Bennett, *Wealth of the Solomons*, 51-58; Stewart Firth, 'German Firms in the Pacific Islands, 1857-1914', In *Germany in the Pacific and Far East, 1870-1914*, ed. J.A. Moses and P. M. Kennedy. (St Lucia: University of Queensland Press, 1972), 7.

3. Chiefs and traders

Johnstone (Sono) and Crossan

Crossan's dealings with his white colleagues (Baker, Darrack, Griffiths) are only hinted at in the Diary, but Johnstone, as Crossan calls Sono, is frequently mentioned and there developed a close if sometimes stormy relationship between the two men. We have some information about Sono from other sources. The Government Agent on *Glencairn* described him as 'the chief of the place' and 'a very decent sort' who spoke English well, having gone away as a boy with Bishop Selwyn of the Melanesian Mission.[1] Sono was one of those from Makira who had gone with Selwyn in the 1850s or early 1860s, probably to Kohimarama, New Zealand, to become a Christian scholar but unlike some others he remained a 'pagan'.[2] Sono was dealing easily with recruiting ships in 1881 when he supplied pigs to Captain Wawn of the *Stanley*. According to Wawn at that time the chief's village was 'a mile or two south of the bay'.[3] By the mid-1880s Sono was also known as 'Johnson' and was described as the chief at Hada Bay.[4]

From Crossan's account it would appear that Johnstone ran the trading station at Hada Bay as almost an equal partner in the business. As the paramount chief at Hada Bay he was the New Zealander's protector, interpreter, and main source of local information. His position is similar to that of Taki, chief of Wango on the north coast, whom the naturalist Henry Guppy encountered in 1882. Taki had 'acquired the double reputation of being a friend to the white man and of being the most accomplished head-hunter in St Christoval' – the one activity obviously facilitating the other.[5] The information in the Crossan journal about Sono gives us more detailed insights into a relationship of growing friendship, trust and mutual dependence between a novice copra trader and a local Makira chief.

In short, the diary provides us with fascinating insights into the process of early colonial contact, seen from the point of view of a 'subaltern' agent of colonialism, William Crossan. In September 1885 this young and inexperienced Otago storekeeper suddenly found himself working, often alone, on the Solomon Islands frontier. The labour trade was in full swing, with recruiters trying to lure

---

1 Pilkington 1885; G. Pilkington, Journal of *Glencairn*, 30 December 1885-14 April 1886, No. 58, NAF.
2 Hilliard, *God's Gentlemen*, 21.
3 Wawn, *The South Sea Islanders and the Queensland Labour Trade*, 247.
4 Cromar, *Jock of the Islands*, 203-4, 252-6, 277; Peter Corris, *Passage, Port and Plantation. A History of Solomon Islands Labour Migration 1870-1914* (Melbourne: Melbourne University Press, 1973), 102.
5 Henry B. Guppy, *The Solomon Islands and their Natives* (London: Swan Sonneschein, 1887), 15.

men away to Queensland and Fiji to work as indentured labour on plantations (Figure 10). In this lawless and liminal world of multiple transactions – of ideas and infections but also tobacco, medicines, gift exchange, political intrigue, sorcery, warfare and cannibalism – Crossan tried to build for himself a new niche as copra trader.

Figure 10. The top-sail schooner *Fearless*, 100 tons, built on Clyde River, New South Wales, in 1876 and registered at Maryborough, Queensland, as a labour recruiting vessel in 1883. The *Fearless* visited Hada Bay in September 1885 soon after Crossan's arrival (see Diary entry for 8th September).

Source: Oxley collection, Queensland State Library.

Crossan as outsider in Solomons

Whatever his feelings about his position within his family back in Otago, in Solomon Islands William Crossan was unequivocally an outsider, yet he seems to have coped with his life there among an unknown and unpredictable people. His youth and robust good health were in his favour. At six months, his stay was very brief, and he lived in a well-ventilated area away from the stagnant waters that provided habitats for *Anopheles* mosquitoes, the vector of malaria. Ned Griffiths who arrived to work in late October was ill with fever by December but he could have contracted the disease on his trip around Malaita. Other white men who resided longer and later than Crossan on this coast soon succumbed to malaria and some almost died of it. In the early 1920s, further east at Waiboroni, a young Englishman in prime physical condition contracted quotidian malaria (*Plasmodium vivax*) after a month and was soon debilitated with consequent depression.[6]

As well as health risks, even after Crossan's time white men along this north west coast had other reasons for concern. Well into the twentieth century the manager at the same plantation at Waiboroni had been fearful and guarded when dealing with bushman, yet in theory the colonial government had administered the Solomons from 1896.[7] Back in 1885-86, apart from occasional cruises by British men-of-war, there was no semblance of state-controlled law and order.

Once ashore on Makira island, Crossan shows an interest in various topics, ranging from shooting birds to baking bread, from earthquakes to tropical cyclones, and from cannibalism to local medicines. First and foremost, however, his diary makes it clear that he was there to work – to construct the Hada Bay store, to build a boat and to make a profit out of copra trading. Because of his robust health and strong work ethic he had little time to become bored. There was a regular traffic in labour vessels calling along the coast from Fiji and Queensland and most brought with them news and newspapers that kept the white traders in touch with doings in the rest of the world. Crossan, although not the most polished of diarists, seemed willing to read anything he could get hold of, from Henry George's *Progress and Poverty* to the Queensland press.

William Crossan was an uninformed and naive observer of Makira affairs, and he often provides us with frustratingly little detail, but what he does record offers some valuable insights into the process of colonialism at micro-scale. His diary provides a fascinating glimpse into the everyday lives of traders and islanders, the means through which newly-colonised Solomon Islanders were being persuaded to produce copra as a commodity for world markets, and the social relations that traders established with big-men like Johnstone. Johnstone was one of the first generation of Melanesian big-men to see opportunities in this strange new world that the white men brought. For Melanesians it was certainly a world of 'guns, germs and steel', as Jared Diamond described Western imperialism,[8] but also a new world of tobacco, missionaries and wage labour in Queensland and Fiji.

---

6 Eric Muspratt, *My South Sea Island* (New York: W. Morrow & Co., 1931), 112.
7 Rigby to Fairley, 16 Sep. 1913, Mumford to Fairley, Fairley, Rigby and Co., 21 May 1914, 25 Dec. 1914, 25 May 1915, Fairley, Rigby Correspondence, University of Melbourne archives, Melbourne.
8 Jared Diamond, *Guns, Germs and Steel. A Short History of Everybody for the Last 13,000 Years* (London: Jonathan Cape, 1997).

Unlike many of those who glimpsed the Solomon Islands, then wrote about them and moved on, men like Crossan were closely engaged with the people for months at a time and had real agency in the areas where they operated. David Hilliard has suggested that 'in cultural impact, the thirty or so traders in the Solomon Islands and the northern New Hebrides in the 'seventies and 'eighties were exceeded only by the labour recruiters'.[9] Many of these resident and itinerant traders in the Solomon Islands were barely literate and kept few records; some perhaps wrote letters or diaries recording their lives in the islands, but without exception nothing that they wrote in this period was published and none of these manuscripts appears to have survived. What we know of these men and their dealings with Melanesians derives from the brief reports of other observers, sometimes hostile. For example, Joseph Atkin, Anglican missionary at Wango on Makira, commented in 1872:

> Whalers and traders often visit these [Solomon] islands; and although of the former, as a class, I have the highest opinion, and think the latter are often judged by the worst specimens; yet still the good the better class do by their visits is far more than counterbalanced by the harm that even one or two really bad ones may do.[10]

Crossan's diary is therefore a rare exception to the usual absence of records, and therefore 'the condescension of history' that is the normal fate of these Islands traders. One pivotal aspect of cultural impact that the diary reveals is the complex relationship between his trading activity and Makira society.

Crossan and Makira society

For all that he was a complete novice, Crossan soon picked up the dominant discourse on Makira Island of a dichotomy within a clan-based and village-based society. He quickly noted the ubiquitous tension between the coastal or saltwater people and the bush people (*tolo/toro*), a dichotomy that soon became evident to all visitors, often to their regret, from the 1840s onwards. When the Marist priests tried to establish a mission to the south at Makira Harbour in 1845-47 they got along reasonably well with the saltwater people, but after the priests made attempts to venture inland the coastal people killed one of their number to keep them confined to the coast so that the coastal people could continue to monopolise their trading contacts with the mission.[11]

---

9   David Hilliard, *God's Gentlemen: A History of the Melanesian Mission, 1849-1942* (St Lucia, Brisbane: University of Queensland Press, 1978), 103.
10 Quoted by Rev. J. J. Halcombe, *Mission Life: An Illustrated Magazine of Home and Foreign Church Work* (London: W. Wells Gardner, 1872), 141. Reprinted by Project Canterbury: http://anglicanhistory.org/oceania/halcombe_atkin1872.html (Accessed 29 January 2011).
11 Laracy, *Marists and Melanesians*, 20-22.

3. Chiefs and traders

There were many other things about Makira's history that Crossan could not have known. Much of the north coast of the island had suffered from at least one major dysentery epidemic that seems to have wiped out whole communities. Variously attributed to a recruiting vessel returning labour or to the visit of the Melanesian Mission's *Southern Cross* in the late 1860s, such a huge loss of life would have re-arranged not only the population but also the politics of the coastal areas, with inland people probably coming down to fill some of the vacant spaces. There were several more waves of an array of introduced diseases to which the local people had little resistance and many died.[12] Crossan noted the presence of venereal disease at Hada Bay, including what seemed to be syphilis which some contemporaries thought resulted from Makira's long history of contacts with whalers and traders as well as the labourers who returned infected from Fiji or Queensland.[13] Crossan probably did not appreciate the negative effects on the birth rate of sexually transmitted diseases, nor how women's sterility contributed greatly to the depopulation of the island.[14] However, a clear recognition of the on-going population decline is implied in his diary entry for 23rd September 1885: 'It is doctors they want down here not missionaries for in the course of a few years if things go on as they are they will be no more natives to instruct in the Bible...'.

All the trade that Crossan carried out was in association with Johnstone, the Hada chief or big-man, and these transactions were confined to the coastal parts of the district. Crossan had no reason to resist this bias as coconuts do not thrive inland but, on the other hand, the Arosi bush people also wanted trade goods and some volunteered to work as labourers for Crossan. Johnstone seems to have tolerated this, perhaps because he had relatives or men from his own totemic clan among them.[15] Probably too Johnstone wanted to see Crossan well settled and close to him, for their mutual benefit. The political subtleties would have been lost on Crossan who would have needed far more than six months to understand the shifting mosaic of inter-clan, inter-village, and inter-regional alliances and conflicts in Arosi alone.

When the bushman killed a man at Lunichena (11th January 1886) the traders at Hada found themselves in the midst of a payback situation, but they seem not to have understood the potential risks. As the local men appeared to have nothing much to do after the months of yam planting from September to December, Crossan seems to have assumed that he could count on them being on hand to

---

12 Kuper to District Officer, 2 Oct. 1933, WPHC F46/35, WPA; Michael W. Scott, *The Severed Snake: Matrilineages, Making Place, and a Melanesian Christianity in Southeast Solomon Islands* (Durham, N.C.: Carolina Academic Press, 2007), 69-103.
13 R. H. Codrington, *The Melanesians* (Oxford: Clarendon Press, 1891), 12.
14 R. A. Herr and E. A. Rood, eds., *A Solomon's Sojourn: J.E. Philp's Log of the Makira 1912-1913* (Hobart: Historical Research Association, 1978), 141.
15 Re totemic clans, see Fox, *The Threshold of the Pacific*, 10-17.

give him help. After the murder at Lunichena Crossan betrays impatience with the Hada men who had become preoccupied with the payback politics of the killing. They would not help him collect copra in his boat and he was even moved to humiliate them in the sight of the bushmen who had come to parley peace. He could have been pushing his luck for Johnstone too was busy with local politics. Though Crossan seems not to have felt any direct repercussions for his show of displeasure with the Hada people, the fact that this stand-off preceded the shooting of a local man by Ned Griffiths almost certainly raised the anxiety levels of both white men.

The bushmen came to Hada on 12th January to cement peace, so they could attack the rest of Lunichena, supposedly without Johnstone's people getting involved. Even so, Crossan went to collect copra from Lunichena, where he noted the people there were away hunting for a bushman in retaliation. These conflicts between bush and saltwater people sometimes were interspersed with alliances and some degree of friendliness, as for example when some of his work boys went to a bush village for several days for 'a big feed' at the time of the full moon, 18th February. But in 1885-86, at least, such friendly relations were not typical and, as far as Crossan was concerned, their occurrence was unpredictable.

Crossan did not speak the Arosi language but he tried to learn it, an indication perhaps that he intended to stay longer than he did or that he had little idea of the difficulty of language learning. He had picked up some pidgin English (Tok Pisin), the language of trade. In some ways Johnstone's knowledge of English (as well as pidgin) meant Crossan and his white companions did not have much need to learn Arosi, but this also meant they were less aware of what was going on around them, were reliant on Johnstone, and always were marginal to Arosi society. One example of how a lack of understanding nearly cost Crossan the support of Johnstone was when he made a coarse remark about Johnstone's 'sister' or close female relative, not realising that in most Melanesian societies talk related to sexuality is totally avoided between and about brothers/sisters or male/female cousins. Such behaviour could lead to conflict or even death. Probably it was Johnstone's tolerance of the ignorance of white men that preserved Crossan, who suffered from nothing more than Johnstone's refusal to speak to him for some time.

Other than his faux pas regarding Johnstone's sister, Crossan had little to say about the Arosi women, but he noted in January 1886 that the wives of two men he knows were ill. He supplied Mai's sick wife with medicine, an act of compassion and also potentially a risk to him if she had died. On 26th September he gave tobacco to the 'Queen' of Ubuna, the wife of the big man, when she along with others from her village took part in a mourning feast for the dead son of Johnstone. As with several other aspects of Arosi culture, Crossan offers hints about the status of women that tantalise the ethnographer. He noted on 28th September that Johnstone's wife had her own new canoe, but perhaps she shared it with her husband and owned only the after part, similar to the recorded custom at Sa'a, south Malaita for canoes used to catch bonito.[16] There is certainly some ritual requirement at work on this occasion since only one fish was allowed to be caught, but Crossan does not elaborate.

Like Darrack after a full day's work, Crossan (30th September) seems to have wished he had a woman to prepare a meal, a function that his mother, a talented cook, must have fulfilled before he left home (and for seventeen years after he returned to his parents' home!). For all this wishing, Crossan appears to have kept his distance from the local women. The 'girls' from Mulhau brought copra to trade, but he does not remark on their appearance in spite of the fact they would have been bare-breasted and partially naked. A contemporaneous observer, the recruiter Jock Cromar claimed that Johnstone had two 'daughters' who soon after were given as wives to the two traders, the Dabelle brothers, but Crossan does not mention these women.[17] They may not have been true daughters in the Western sense, but classificatory ones – nieces or adoptees – a category of Arosi kinship that would have not been obvious to Crossan.[18]

Within a month on Makira, though at times he was inadvertently clumsy, Crossan was increasingly willing to participate in the culture. Most opportunities to take part in customary exchanges were grasped in order perhaps to gain acceptance as a trader or simply to identify with his new community and support Johnstone. In October, he contributed tobacco and matches to the crew of the new war canoe from Lunichena as it toured along the coast. He regularly gave presents to Johnstone out of friendship as well as business. While never participating in cannibalism he seemed less disturbed by it as he saw more examples and certainly, if he were disgusted, he did not reveal this to his Arosi hosts.

The dangers of the middle ground

In Crossan's time and beyond, Johnstone had an advantage that few other big-men had - he had spent time at the Melanesian Mission in New Zealand, seemed to have had well-travelled male relatives, and had a good grasp of the labour trade as well as the copra trade. He knew what the white men needed, but he was too intelligent to be their minion. Moreover, Johnstone was far from being a lazy or exploitative middle-man. Displaying the characteristic enterprise of a big-man, he was hard-working and co-operated with Crossan on most of his projects, from boat building to actual copra drying.

---

16   Walter Ivens, *Melanesians of the South-East Solomons* (London: Kegan Paul, Trench, Trubner & Co., 1927), 144.
17   Cromar, *Jock of the Islands*, 255-256.
18   Fox, *The Threshold of the Pacific*, 17-20.

Even so, on this cusp of intercultural space, Johnstone's position could have been somewhat marginalized through his association with traders such as Crossan. Quite early on Crossan sensed that islanders who were outside the Hada faction resented Johnstone's easy contact with the traders and their useful knowledge about such things as repairing firearms. In his diary entry on 13th September Crossan notes:

> There is great enmity between Johnstone's crowd & the other natives. They all seem to be very jealous of white men staying here [in Hada]. The chief [at Tawaraha] offered me a nice piece of ground if I would come and stop.

These islanders may have been envious of Johnstone's ready access to traded goods such as tobacco, matches and cloth – all of which could make life a little easier. He had to tread a careful path between placating his followers and doing what was needed to keep 'his traders' on side.

For his part, Crossan also had to be careful about maintaining relationships with other white men. Unlike the recruiter William Wawn who knew Makira, Crossan reflects none of the antipathy between labour recruiters and on-shore traders.[19] This may have been because of his utter dependence on the recruiting ship *Glencairn* and on the brief social contact with his own people that the recruiting ships brought. Nonetheless, in regard to other traders, he was careful. He seems to have accepted the informal boundaries that they maintained among themselves and did not do business with the agents that other traders had established in particular areas. Yet this balance, like the balance of loyalties within indigenous society, could also shift in the face of strong incentives. We see an example of such a shift four years later, when Tom Dabelle was murdered at Anuta in March 1889.[20]

Tom Dabelle, before he moved to Anuta Island off the south coast of Arosi district in early 1889, had set up a station just south of Johnstone's village in Hada Bay, at Tawaraha and he seems to have worked with him, just as Crossan had. After his brother went to trade at Simbo in the Western Solomons, Tom Dabelle left Johnstone's area because his own trade store did not have a good beach landing and because the Anuta people invited him to come south to them.[21] Both Johnstone and Tom Dabelle traded with Waterhouse, a Sydney trader. A rival firm of Kelly and Williams employed Woodhouse and another trader, Keating. After Dabelle's murder these two - Woodhouse and Keating - convinced the commander of the British warship *Royalist* that Johnstone was

---

19 Wawn, *The South Sea Islanders*, 223, 286, 344.
20 Bennett, *Wealth of the Solomons*, 55-56.
21 The recruiter Cromar claimed Tom Dabelle moved because he did not like Johnstone's insistence that he and his daughter shared not only the trader's table, but also his house (Cromar, *Jock of the Islands*, 238).

behind the killing, so much so, that the warship shelled Johnstone's village as an 'act of war'. The British warships patrolled these waters supposedly to protect and supervise British subjects, but they had no authority over the native people so had to employ the gloss of declaring war to punish those they judged to have injured white men. The *Royalist*'s commander came to believe the murderer was Johnstone, in part because he was found to have some of Dabelle's possessions removed from Anuta. Johnstone was taken aboard the *Royalist* but he accused two other men of being the killers. Soon after, he was imprisoned in Cooktown in Queensland pending trial. Later, another trader Sam Craig, then unconnected to the rival firms, stated that Dabelle was killed by local Anuta people because he, along with Johnstone, had assisted another British warship in tracking down the murderers of another trader, Bevan, in 1888.

The Anglican missionary Richard Comins then intervened. Comins had worked intermittently for many years in the region but was no particular admirer of the former convert and lapsed student of Christianity, Johnstone. Nonetheless, he insisted Johnstone had been falsely accused, pointing out that for many years Johnstone had been a friend and protector of white men and that he would have damaged his own business if he had ever hurt any of them. Comins was determined to see justice done and returned to Makira to talk with villagers, many of whom he knew well. He found that the two men that Johnstone had named were in fact bushmen staying at coastal Rumahui, south of Hada. They had been paid by a bush chief to kill a white man in revenge for the death of the chief's son who had been recruited by a labour ship. Johnstone had learned of the killing the day after and had rescued Dabelle's goods to prevent pillage. This upset the Anuta people who seem to have already begun to help themselves. Eventually, Johnstone was released for lack of evidence and assisted in the search for the two killers, at least one of whom the British subsequently hanged. John Stephens, an experienced trader based at Uki, held that Johnstone knew about the plot by these men and could have warned Dabelle. Whatever the truth, the rivalry of traders could endanger a big-man like Johnstone as much as local jealousy of his status. Life in the Solomons was often tenuous.[22]

Although Crossan was busy much of the time with building and trading, he had to grapple with similar ambiguities and risks associated with the trader's role as intruder into an alien culture. The diary reflects these anxieties and contradictions. On the one hand, he considers the local people 'Niggers' and seems surprised at the fatherly feelings Johnstone has for a sick and dying son. Within the same diary entry he is repulsed by the personal filth of the natives and the sickness of some, yet he notes that they were dying out and considers it 'a great pity as they are a fair class of people.' When he does not like the idea of the child in its coffin being inside Johnstone's house he tries to

---

22   WPHC 191/89, 82/1890, 125/1890, 158/1890, 230/1890, 96/1891, WPA.

persuade Johnstone to bury the child. He nonetheless shows compassion for the mourning father with gifts of rum and food and finds that Johnstone too 'is really very kind and considerate towards us,' implying that he sees and shares a common humanity.

Selective quotation from this diary could be used to sustain various alternative narratives about the nature of colonialism, but taken as a whole it reminds us that the process was complex, contingent and subject to all the whims and contradictions of our own everyday lives.

William Crossan chronicles all these aspects of his life on Makira in plain, factual language and generally with good humour, but he also expresses to his silent *socius* occasional feelings of alarm, disgust, boredom and frustration. In the last two months the diary entries become shorter and less informative, until early March 1886 when the entries come to an abrupt end as Crossan suddenly decides to return to New Zealand, possibly in fear of his life because of a careless, perhaps criminal, shooting incident at Hada Bay for which his partner Ned Griffiths was responsible. Crossan survived his six months in Solomon Islands and so did his diary. It has been preserved in Dunedin's Hocken Library archives since 1987 and now, through the internet, it can be published to a much wider audience than Crossan himself could ever have imagined.

4. Crossan's Hada Bay Diary

The manuscript

William Crossan's diary is to be found within a softbound notebook that also contains two photographs. One we presume is a portrait of the author (see Figure 2); another shows a worn copy of a group of Solomon Islanders and has the handwritten caption 'Natives at Fatuaa 1889', being a studio portrait with set costume props. It may have been collected by Crossan as a souvenir (Figure 11).[1] These documents are all classified by the Hocken Library as follows: Hocken Library, Misc-MS-1224. WILLIAM J. CROSSAN, DIARY.

The transcript that follows adopts all Crossan's abbreviations and eccentricities of spelling. The word 'of' is often used where 'off' is intended, and 'to' and 'too' are often used interchangeably. Crossan wrote his diary in pencil from September 3rd until 6th November, and thereafter in pen and ink. The entries made in pencil are faint and Crossan's hand-writing is sometimes difficult to read. In the transcript the word [*illegible*] indicates where there is an occasional word or words that cannot be deciphered. Elsewhere in the notebook there are a few lists and recipes also written in Crossan's hand. Some of these clearly date from the Hada Bay period, and where relevant we reproduce them in the footnotes.

Punctuation is generally absent in the diary, full-stops and commas are hard to distinguish, and capital letters are generally not used at the beginning of sentences. This version is a verbatim transcript but to enhance its legibility we have added some punctuation: a few commas, full stops where the end of a sentence is clearly intended, and an initial capital letter to all the words that begin sentences. In his daily entries, where Crossan has not indicated the month we have added this information, e.g. [September]. However, we have not corrected his dates even where his reckoning of time repeats a day and becomes inaccurate – for example, Crossan and Griffith celebrated Christmas Day on what was actually 24th December, but 'December 25th' is the uncorrected date in the version that follows.

---

1 Brigitte d'Ozouville, 'F. H. Dufty in Fiji, 1871-92: The Social Role of the Colonial Photographer in Fiji'. *History of Photography* 1997, 21, 1: 32-41.

Figure 11. A photograph entitled 'Natives at Fatuaa, 1889' found inside the Crossan diary-notebook. It is probably a studio portrait of Malaitans taken in Fiji by Dufty Brothers, and kept by Crossan as a souvenir of his days in Solomon Islands. There seems to be no village of that name today on Malaita. The word 'fatuaa' in the Kwara'ae language may refer to a special gathering or feast and the men are wearing finery for dancing suited to such an occasion.

Source: Re 'fatuaa', Sam Alasia.

Transcript of the Diary

Solomon Islands

Hada Bay

September Thursday 3rd 85[2]

Went on board schr[3] got a few medicines, schr departed Bay same day for Mackerie.[4]

In afternoon marked of stores & arranged them all ready for trade. Johnstone out & caught fish. Went out & shot pigeons.[5] Fowls got out of Box.[6]

---

2   Crossan arrived at Hada Bay on 28th August but he did not begin his diary until 3rd September when his house was completed, the party's stores were all unloaded from *Glencairn* and the ship itself departed. The first Hada Bay record, however, is written on another page of the notebook. It is a list of 'General Expenses' showing that on 2nd September 57 sticks of tobacco were expended on 'Labor':

'Sept 2	57 Tobacco	Labor
Sept 3	35 Tobacco	Labor
Sept 3	5 Tobacco	Yam's
Sept 3	4 Tobacco	Labor
Sept 5	2 Tobacco	Yam's
Sept 6	1 Beef 1/-, 1 Knife 1/-, 2 Turkey Twill 2/-	Johnny
Sept 6	1 tob	Wood
Sept 10th	30 tob Bushman Copra House to be paid when house finished *[this line crossed out]*	
Sept 12	12	Boat crew
Sept 12	150	Bushman copra house'

Apart from the final payment for the copra house the biggest payments in this list were on 2nd and 3rd September when 57 and 35 sticks of tobacco were paid for labour, probably for house building and the unloading of stores. It is unclear what payment if any was made for the land, but already on 6th September special gifts were being made to 'Johnny', presumably Johnstone. Crossan's list shows that tobacco was the most general form of currency in Solomon Islands at this time. It was not until the turn of the century that some islanders began to demand cash for their goods, land and labour (Bennett, *Wealth of the Solomons*, 54).

3   'schr' is the schooner *Glencairn*, 62 tons, built at Auckland of kauri pine (see Figure 9). Before reaching Hada Bay the *Glencairn* had visited Uki on 26th August 1885, where it met up with three other ships at anchor there: the schooner *Venture*, the *Ripple* (a steamer trading to and from Sydney), and the Melanesian Mission ship *Southern Cross* (G. Pilkington, Journal of *Glencairn*, No. 56, 1 August-8 December 1885, Government Agents Journals, NAF). After 1892 *Glencairn* was employed transporting timber around the coasts of New Zealand until September 1900 when the ship was wrecked in a storm on Ninety Mile Beach (*Timaru Herald* vol. 64, no. 3384, 2 October 1900).

4   'Mackerie' is one of many ways that Crossan misspelt 'Makira'. Makira Harbour lies 30 km southwest of Hada Bay, and had been favoured by visiting whaling ships since the 1820s and by deserters and castaways since at least 1851 (Bennett, *Wealth of the Solomons*, 356-7). In 1871 W. Perry established a trading station there that continued until his death three years later (Edwin Redlich, 'Notes on the western islands of the Pacific Ocean and New Guinea', *Journal of the Royal Geographical Society* 1874, 44, 30-37). John Stephens was resident trader at Makira from 1876 until the following year when the station closed and Stephens moved to Uki, which became the central place in a network that extended westwards as far as Ubuna. Stanley Bateman and/or his two brothers reopened the Makira station in 1880 (Bennett, *Wealth of the Solomons*, 376-7).

5   The pigeons Crossan shot were probably a species of Imperial-Pigeon, *Ducula* spp. Woodford reported that in the Solomon Islands 'every island swarms with large fruit pigeons' (Charles Woodford, *A Naturalist among the Headhunters: being an Account of Three Visits to the Solomon Islands in the Years 1886, 1887 and 1888* (London: George Philip & Sons, 1890), 56). In 1865 Englishmen visiting the island shot numerous pigeons including the Chestnut-bellied Imperial-Pigeon (*Ducula brenchleyi*) at Wango and Hada Bay (J. Brenchley, *Jottings during the cruise of H.M.S. Curaçoa among the South Sea Islands in 1865* (London: Longman, Green & Co., 1873), 388).

6   The New Zealand party seems to have brought with them their own hens as a source of food as well as a pig (which died) and the dog Rover.

Friday 4th [September]

Got up 6 a.m., had bath. Men finished cook house. Shot 2 crains[7] in evening. Pig died.

Saturday 6th [September][8]

Rose early. Finished cook house, made bread, sent men to bush for timber for door's.[9]

Made door for house. Bought yam's.[10] Bushmen gave us a visit, quite friendly.[11] Johnstone made a failure of catching fish. Native gave us 3 for breakfast. Cut 3 boys hair, seemed to amuse the natives very much. Johnstone gave us the native idea of cannabalism, when a Bushman is killed & they get the corpse, it is a valuable commodity as trade. They pay the highest price for a very small piece for food & will do nearly anything to procure it.[12]

---

7   There are no cranes ('crains') in Solomon Islands but the Pacific Reef Egret *Egretta sacra* is a not dissimilar bird, and is common along shorelines.
8   Crossan here jumps a day in his reckoning of dates, writing 6th not 5th September. He continues with this mistake until Monday 20th October when he corrects it, only to repeat the same mistake on Friday 7th November and thereafter.
9   This timber ('wood') was paid for with one stick of tobacco, according to the separate list that Crossan made of his 'General Expenses' (see footnote to 3rd September).
10   This is the first of several references by Crossan to 'yams', *Dioscorea* spp., which were still the primary staple at this time. John Cromar (*Jock of the Islands*, 147) visited Makira on labour recruiting ships in the 1880s and wrote that 'San Cristobal Island was renowned for its pannas, a kind of small yam that resembled a floury potato when baked' ('pana' is Tok Pisin for the Sweet Yam, *D. esculenta*). It is striking that nowhere in his account does Crossan mention sweet potato and cassava, the modern staples. Sweet potato, or 'kumara' in Tok Pisin, is a plant not native to the Solomons, and it probably was first introduced to the islands by returning mission 'scholars', ship's crew or labourers. If present at all on Makira at this time, it was clearly not prominent.
11   'Bushmen' refer to the people of the interior. The bush/coastal distinction was already very marked when Marist priests from France first tried to establish a foothold on the island at Makira Harbour in 1845 (Laracy, *Marists and Melanesians*, 21). Guppy noted that 'the large island of St Christoval is divided amongst numerous tribes between which there are constant feuds, each tribe having its own chief. A wide distinction exists between the inhabitants of the interior and those of the coast; and an unceasing hostility prevails between the one and the other' (Guppy, *The Solomon Islands and their Natives*, 14).
12   These anecdotes about cannibalism certainly reflect Crossan's naivety and they might also be seen as reflecting the ignorant and stereotyped views prevalent among the white population of Solomon Islands at this time, perhaps especially among New Zealanders who were disdainful of Maori cultural practices. Probably, however, they truthfully reflect the prevailing situation. Robert Codrington (*The Melanesians* (Oxford: Clarendon Press, 1891), 344), an Anglican missionary, linguist and ethnologist, provides a similar account based on repeated visits that he made to Makira (San Cristoval) in the 1870s: 'The natives of San Cristoval not only eat the bodies of those who are slain in battle, but sell the flesh. To kill for the purpose of eating flesh, though not unknown, is rare, and is a thing which marks the man who has done it. This is a subject on which stories that come from traders are not very trustworthy'. Following his visits to north Makira in 1882-83, Guppy confirms that cannibalism mainly took place in ritual contexts, such as the completion of a new tambu-house: 'If the victim is not procured in a raid amongst the neighbouring tribes of the interior, some man is usually selected from those men of the village who were originally purchased [for adoption] by the chief'. Dr Guppy's information came from white traders like Bateman and Stephens, from local informants, and also from his own identification of the cannibalised leg and arm bones of human victims, alongside pig bones, that he saw adorning tambu-houses (Guppy, *The Solomon Islands and their Natives*, 35-37).

Johnstone sent off his copra to Tunins cutter, told us Tunin was to pay us a visit.[13] Up to the present 6.30 p.m. has not arrived. Tunin, in trying to sort the King's Snidher[14] at Buna, shot the King, & there is a price put on his head. He is afraid to go to Buna.[15]

Freeman an American some long time ago, the natives of this town & the Bushmen had a Row, the natives headed by Freeman, went & had a fight. Freeman shot a Bushman & received the native pay, & they had a good cannabill feast.[16]

Sunday 7th September 85

Rose 6.30, had coffee, got bath, wrote a lot of native words down to try & learn the language.[17] 10 a.m. had breakfast. Johnstone away to catch fish. Topsail schooner sighted abt 1 p.m., anchored in Hada Bay. 4 p.m. 2 boats came ashore,

---

13   This statement shows that Sono (hereafter called Johnstone) was not only the Hada Bay chief but was also a trading middleman, collecting copra by means of local exchange or the efforts of his Hada Bay faction, and then selling it directly to 'Tunin' whose identity is unclear. 'Tunin' is unlikely to be a garbled version of 'Comins', Stephen Comins being the Anglican missionary responsible for the school at Heuru, as such people would never repair firearms and were not engaged in copra trading. It seems most probable that 'Tunin' is Johnstone's version of the name 'John Stephens'. Stephens was one of the earliest traders in Solomon Islands and traded at Savo and Guadalacanal in 1870 before settling at Uki Island. Between 1871 and 1882 he bought 2,000 acres of land on Uki, but his main business was buying copra and selling trade goods, notably firearms. He died on Uki about 1893 (Corris, *Passage, Port and Plantation*, 99; Graeme Golden, *The Early European Settlers of the Solomon Islands* (Mentone, Melbourne, 1993), 274-275). 'Steve's cutter' is mentioned in the diary again on 24th and 25th September, but it appears that Crossan and Stephens never met.
14   'Snidher' is the Snider rifle, an important item of trade since about 1878. Judith Bennett (*Wealth of the Solomons*, 88) comments that the acquisition of new guns in the 1880s made Solomon Islands warriors much more effective: 'Snider breech loaders, Martini-Henry rifles, and the occasional Winchester rifle began by the 1880s to supersede the inferior single-shot muskets'. In 1885 one Snider cost £3 or about 6,000 coconuts, which was three times the price of a musket (Bennett, *Wealth of the Solomons*, 81). In 1884, however, both Fiji and Queensland responded to pressure from the British Government by making the trade in firearms, gunpowder and ammunition illegal for British nationals, and forbidding the transport of guns by labourers returning from plantation labour (much to their disgust, see Cromar, *Jock of the Islands*, 113-114). Germans, French and Americans were not bound by these rules and continued to trade in Snider rifles, other weapons and ammunition (Charles M. Woodford, 'Exploration of the Solomon Islands', *Proceedings of the Royal Geographical Society* 10, 1888, 351-376).
15   The King of Buna is alluded to several times in the diary, and refers to the paramount big-man or chief residing in Ubuna on the north coast, about 20 km east from Hada Bay. For a while Ubuna had also been a trading station, established in 1877 by a German called Fred Howard who used Ubuna as his base before he upset the local people and had to move to Uki. The King may well have been a man called Donasu, a leader in the estimation of the missionary R. B. Comins (Comins to High Commissioner, 26 July 1890, WPHC 230/90, WPA).
16   The identity of Freeman is unknown, but this story could relate to one of the American castaways who were living at Hada Bay in 1865 (Rietmann, *Wanderungen in Australien und Polynesien*, 183-4). In 1876 the schooner *Dancing Wave* (Captain Davis) called at Hada Bay 'and took on board a settler named Freeman' who then became the vessel's trading master. After calling at Guadalcanal and Savo the *Dancing Wave* went to Nggela for pearl shell, and was attacked by the islanders. Freeman was one of the first to be killed with a tomahawk (*Clarence and Richmond Examiner and New England Advertiser*, 10 July 1976, 2).
17   There is no record in the diary notebook of these lists of words which must have been in the Arosi language, this being the language of the north-west part of Makira Island (Robert Codrington, *The Melanesian Languages*, (Oxford: Clarendon Press, 1885), 505; Charles Fox, *Arosi Dictionary, Revised Edition* (Canberra: The Australian National University, 1978)). Indeed, during all his trading voyages in the following six months Crossan never operated outside the Arosi area. This restriction is partly a reflection of the pre-existing territories of his trading competitors on Uki Island and in Makira Bay. However, it may also reflect the influence of Johnstone and his Hada Bay employees ('boys'), none of whom would have been comfortable journeying outside their language area.

landed 1 woman, 2 men. Govt. Agent[18] Mr White & Supercargo came to house & had refreshments. Promised us some papers in morning. Went on with boats to land man higher up. 15 days from Maryborough to Santa Anna, all well.[19]

Monday 8th September 85

Rose 5.30 p.m., bath, breakfast early, went on board the Topsail Schooner Feerless,[20] Capt. Prock,[21] Mr Turner 'mate',[22] Mr Jones Govt Agt.[23] Had dinner on board, & Govt Agt. gave me a number of Queensland papers. Came ashore abt 3.30 p.m. with schooner's boat. They procured some yams. One Guadalcanar boy deserted from the ship.[24] A very nice lot off people on board & treated us very well. Mr Turner gave me an illustration of what an Obah chief thought of the Miranda's H.B.M.'s man of war.[25] He looked at some of the big guns and said to the Captain 'that good fellow Snider, no gammon belong him, you get him Maryborough'.[26] Had tea, read a few papers & went to bed 8 p.m. Johnstone up all last night looking out for Bushman, makee fight.

---

18 From 1871 any ship recruiting labour for the Queensland plantations was required to have on board a government agent (G.A.), whose job it was to prevent abuses and to make sure that recruits understood the terms of the labour contract (both of them difficult if not impossible tasks). The Second Pacific Islanders' Protection Act of 1875 applied the same regulations to Fiji, which had become a British colony the previous year. The phrase 'landed one woman, two men' refers to labourers returned by *Fearless* to the area where they had been recruited, as the law required.

19 Maryborough is in Queensland, Australia; Santa Ana is a small island off the eastern tip of Makira.

20 The *Fearless* was described by Cromar (*Jock of the Islands*, 238) as 'a topsail schooner of one hundred tons register' (see Figure 10). It was built in 1876 on the Clyde River, N.S.W., and in March 1883 was registered in Maryborough, Queensland as a labour recruiting vessel, length 86 feet, breadth 21 feet and with draught 8 ft 7 ins. *Fearless* was wrecked on San Cristoval on 21st January 1902 (Patere Ioane, *Kanaka Marau. A Sociopolitical Drama about the Economy of a Colony 1899-1902* (Tenaru, Solomon Islands: St Joseph's School, 1993), 35).

21 The hand writing is unclear, and the captain's name could be Pasck or Praek. In early or mid-1885 there was a Captain Pasch in charge of the labour recruiter *Storm Bird* (Cromar, *Jock of the Islands*, 146), while in 1893 the owner of *Fearless* was a man called Augustus Paech (Ioane, *Kanaka Marau*, 35). Either of these could be the same man as Crossan's Prock/Pasck/Praek.

22 This man was John Turner, described by Cromar (*Jock of the Islands*, 157) as 'a Greek who had a brother, Agislaus Turnaros whom I already knew. He [Turner] and his brother had both been miners, but had taken up navigation and obtained their master's certificates... [Turner's] left leg was bowed and made his gait a crooked one; he made a droll figure hobbling along in a Greek petticoat that he wore...He spoke a queer mixture of *beche-de-mer* [Pidgin English], English and Greek or Italian that was easily enough understood when one became used to it, but it sounded strange to unaccustomed ears'. In the following year, 1886, John Turner was captain of the labour recruiting schooner *Helena* and once again visited Hada Bay (see Diary, 5th February) and Makira Harbour.

23 'Mr Jones' is a different name from the 'Mr White' who Crossan had identified as the Government Agent the previous evening.

24 'Guadalcanar' is the island of Guadalcanal, a popular recruiting ground for blackbirders and evidently a place that *Fearless* had already visited prior to its arrival at Hada Bay. In some cases, for example if in some kind of trouble at home, a returning islander would choose to be landed in another place even though it was against regulations for a captain to do so even if requested. Alternatively a returned labourer might run away far from his home, as in this case.

25 'Obah' is probably Aoba Island in New Hebrides, where *Miranda* was investigating labour recruitment in 1884-5. Her Britannic Majesty's Ship *Miranda* was an Osprey class sloop built in 1879 and decommissioned in 1892. During the 1880s *Miranda* was attached to the Western Pacific High Commission in Fiji and spent her time investigating disputes and outrages in the South Pacific, for example the attack on H.M.S. *Sandfly* in Nggela, Solomon Islands, in 1881.

26 The reported comment indicates the high status of Snider rifles at this time, and is evidence too for the early use of Pidgin English in a form quite similar to Tok Pisin today.

4. Crossan's Hada Bay Diary

Tuesday 9th September 85

Rose early, Johnstone caught Mackerill, got 2 pigeons, washed clothes. Feerless left early in morning. Took posts out of forest, ready to start boat building in morning.[27] Johnstone looking after sick infant. Guadalcanar boy turned up in the evening.[28] Weather cloudy.

Wednesday 10 Sept 85

Rose early 5.30 a.m. Went & seen Johnstone to go to Buna, but the rain was to heavy, put it of til 11th. Had breakfast early & started preparations for boat. Got bench up, grindstone set & everything in order for a start. Heavy surf rolling in, weather cloudy & close in the afternoon. Worked till late. 10 bushman building copra house all day. Boy out & shot 5 pigeons. Men want paid for house when finished, they seem to put more confidence in us now.[29] Got things ready for breakfast, & sorted out trade for morning. Our Boy Johnie looks after the house splendid, when we are out, lets nobody in.

I tried Waiho with a shot out of the Snider, when he fired it of he was looking one way & the rifle another. The natives bring in an endless variety of guns & pistols for repair, but they are all to much matie matie.[30] Had bath in evening. Feel tired and will now turn in, 7.30 p.m.

Thursday 11 Sept 85

Rose very early, got boat ready, & started with Johnstone & 5 men for Buna.[31] Had a good day, seen plenty of coconut on the way down at Marowe Harbor. No natives living there.[32] Bushmen come down occasionally. Johnstone told me that he shot a Bush woman & sold the corpse to the King of Buna & they

---

27 Crossan and Darrack realised that not having a cutter of their own severely limited the company's access to trading opportunities beyond Hada Bay, so that constructing this boat becomes a high priority. The task was to occupy Crossan, Darrack, Johnstone and others on most days during the eight-week period from 10th September until 5th November 1885. Darrack had some boatbuilding skills, presumably derived from the boatbuilding business run by members of the Darrack family in Auckland (*Daily Southern Cross*, 30 September 1875, 2).
28 A man from Guadalcanal would have had no kinship connections on Makira, and his main hope of survival was to attach himself to a foreign missionary or trading station.
29 Up to this point, it would appear that labourers had been paid at the end of each day's work. The rate of pay was reckoned in sticks of twist tobacco, as money was not yet in general use. Charles Woodford travelled widely in Solomon Islands in 1886-87, and stated that '[t]he chief article of exchange between traders and natives is tobacco, of which the natives are very fond and are pretty good judges, while pipes, wax matches, calico, beads, necklaces, Jews harps, knives and axes are also bought' (Woodford, 'Exploration of the Solomon Islands', 354)
30 The phrase 'matie matie' is probably Crossan's rendering of the Arosi word 'maitaita' which means 'broken' (Fox, *Arosi Dictionary*, 270).
31 Ubuna is 10 km northeast from Hada Bay, past Maro'u Bay along the north coast. Crossan used what he later called 'the small boat', probably a whale-boat with six oars, hence the six Solomon Islanders (including Johnstone) who travelled with him and the 'long pull' on the way back. Such craft were slow and had limited cargo capacity, which explains Crossan's determination to construct a bigger sailing boat that he could use as a cutter.
32 Marowe Harbour is now called Maro'u Bay. Thirty years later, in 1913, the copra trader J.E. Philp noted the presence there of several cemeteries and commented 'Maru Bay was at one time densely populated'. By

had a very big tom tom or feast over the occasion. This Buna King and his subordinates look the very picture of cannabals.[33] I dined with the King today & at his request had to eat out of the same pot as himself. My appetite failed me very much, but to please him I eat a little yam. A number of the men were away at Uigi drying copra for tobacco.[34] They were all out of the weed, and us getting there at the time we did suited them admirably. I left a quantity of trade for the king to purchase copra with, left there abt 2 p.m. & got home abt 9 p.m. after a little difficulty in getting the boat anchored. Very tired, long pull. I will sleep well tonight, had not such an appetite for many a long day.

Friday 12th September 85

Started cut stem & stern posts for boat. Finished them in evening. Cut my finger. Boy shot 7 pigeons. Day very warm. Put copra out to dry. Paid bushmen for making house. Noticed new moon first time yesterday evening. Strong wind blowing outside. Adopted the sulu costume for wearing in the evening.[35] Had good bath and feell quite satisfied with progress made.

Saturday 13th September 1885

Started boat first thing. Had breakfast. Packed up trade and went over to Sandy's place. Bought a little copra. Sandy bought some flour.[36] There is great enmity between Johnstone's crowd & the other natives. They all seem to be very jealous

---

1913 it was the site of a coconut plantation and trade store run by Dick Richardson, an Afro-American from Baltimore (R.A. Herr and E.A. Rood, eds., *A Solomons Sojourn: J.E. Philp's Log of the Makira, 1912-1913* (Hobart: Tasmanian Historical Research Association, 1978), 132).

33   Crossan was not pre-disposed to regard the Ubuna chief as trustworthy, and he was no doubt aware of the incident in August 1880 when the resident trader there was Stanley Bateman. According to Bennett (*Wealth of the Solomons*, 67) 'the mate of the *Venture*, while in a whaleboat with resident trader Bateman off Ubuna, accidentally shot a big-man, Aurua, who was with him when his gun misfired. The captain, Wolsch, set sail for Sydney but Bateman, at considerable personal risk, chose to return to the village to explain events and conciliate the people'. In 1882 Guppy was also told about a fatal accident, probably the same one, 'about a year before ... on board a trading-vessel through a revolver going off unexpectedly'. As a result 'we learned that there was head-money out for a white man's head in a district on the north side and nearly opposite Ugi... It was the current opinion of resident traders that sooner or later the required head would be obtained' (Guppy, *The Solomon Islands and their Natives*, 17).

34   Uki Island had been the base for numerous white traders starting in 1868 (Bennett, *Wealth of the Solomons*, 376-8). From about 1871 until 1890 John Stephens resided there, selling trade goods especially firearms, and shipping his copra to Cowlishaw Brothers, later Waterhouse Co., in Sydney. Stephens purchased about 2,000 acres of land on Uki between 1871 and 1882, but only about 5 acres of land around his house was ever developed. Fred Howard worked for Stephens as a trader at Uki from 1880 to 1891, when he was killed by Malaita men contracted by the Uki chief Rora. The reason was that Howard had apparently objected to the Uki people making copra from coconuts growing on the area of land previously 'sold' to Stephens (Kaye Green, 'A history of post-Spanish European contact in the Eastern District before 1939', in R.C. Green and M. Cresswell, eds., *Southeast Solomon Islands Cultural History* (Wellington: Royal Society of New Zealand), 1976, 38; Golden, *The Early European Settlers*, 274-5).

35   A sulu is a wrap-around skirt about a metre wide worn around the waist. This is a Fijian term and suggests that Crossan had already spent some time in Fiji.

36   Sandy was a local trader living close to Hada Bay, possibly at Tawaraha about 3 km south of Hada Bay. The transaction reported here, copra being exchanged for flour, is an example of the barter arrangements through which a network of traders and their local agents was maintained.

of white men staying here. The chief offered me a nice piece of ground if I would come and stop.[37] Strong wind blowing, the boys got a little frightened at the sail, & took it down. Day warm. Boy shot 1 pigeon. Johnstone worked hard at the boat.

Sunday 14th September 85

Had a good lay in bed, no work today. George made a good plum duff[38] & passed the day in laziness.[39] Canoe came from Buna, also man from Sandy's settlement for trade. Good prospect of plenty of copra coming in. Another failure in bread baking.[40] Johnstone says when he kills one more man belonging to the Bush then he will become a missionary.[41] Day very warm, strong breeze blowing from SW.

Monday 15th [September] 85

Rose early, breakfast at 10. Cut knees and other wood for boat. Got keel set up. Baked some bread & had a general days cooking. Day warm, strong wind. Wilhara in bush looking out his yam ground.[42] Johnstone hard at work. Boy shot 4 pigeons. Had dinner at 7 p.m., retired early.

---

37 Inducements of this kind were common at this time, as the presence of a white man meant trade and often guns, although after 1884 British subjects in the islands were not supposed to trade in firearms or ammunition. According to Cromar, '[h]enceforth the time-expired kanakas from Queensland took their wages back to the islands with them, and there purchased all the firearms they desired from the local traders and non-British vessels' masters' (Cromar, (*Jock of the Islands*, 113).
38 Plum duff was originally a sailor's name for plum pudding, probably derived from 'plum dough'. It is a misnomer as these boiled puddings never contained plums and seldom even prunes. Their basic fruit was currants and the fat was suet. There was generally no raising agent so the pudding was very dense. The mixture was tied up in a floured wet cloth and cooked in a large boiler for several hours (Prof. Helen Leach, University of Otago, personal communication, 2011).
39 Crossan has a mixed relationship with George, who appears to be a permanent member of Johnstone's faction at Hada Bay. Two months later on 21st December George punches Crossan's house boy and is banished, but in the diary he reappears at the end of January suffering from malaria and is given medicine.
40 No doubt a great disappointment, as Crossan came from a family of bakers – his stepfather was a baker (see 'William Crossan's Life', this volume).
41 The phrase 'become a missionary' refers to the practices of the Melanesian Mission. The Mission hoped its male converts would become pastors, and this was the intended career path of men like Johnstone who had been taken away as boys for schooling on Norfolk Island. No white missionaries were present in the Hada Bay area at this time, but since 1870 there had been a Melanesian Mission school on the north coast at Wango, there was another at Fagani (Ha'ani) that began about the same time, and a third school was started at Heuru by the Melanesian pastor William Duru in 1882. Despite this effort, the first baptisms did not take place until 1875 and in 1894 there were still only 135 Christians in total on the whole island (Charles Fox, *Lord of the Southern Isles, being the Story of the Anglican Mission in Melanesia 1849-1949* (London: A.R. Mowbray, 1958), 160).
42 The two yam species *Dioscorea esculenta* and *D. alata* were cultivated together on Makira, in a swidden cycle that involved planting on a newly cleared plot in September-October and harvesting in March-April. The harvested yams were stored in special houses (Douglas Yen, 'Agricultural systems and prehistory in the Solomon Islands', in R.C. Green and M. Cresswell, eds., *Southeast Solomon Islands Cultural History* (Wellington: Royal Society of New Zealand, 1976), 63).

Tuesday 16th September

Rose early, breakfast at 10 a.m. Worked at boat all day. Natives all in bush planting yams. Johnstone looking after his child very sick. George & a lot of natives came this evening. Day warm, strong SE wind blowing. Boy Illimo refused to go for water, he is a lazy young d-- .

Wednesday 17th Sept

Rose at daylight, had breakfast at 10 a.m., got starboard streak on boat. Queensland Brigantine Helena (Labor) from New Hebrides with 65 recruits on board sighted abt 1 p.m. anchored in Hada Bay.[43] 2 boats came ashore to buy yams. 4 white men came to house, and had refreshments & went on.[44]

[page missing]

Saturday 20th September

Started and worked at boat first thing in the morning, got 2 planks when Darrack had to knock of owing to his back being so very bad. Kidney complaint I think, he can hardly move this afternoon. Rubbed it with St Jacob's oil & gave salt pitre.[45] Had a good dinner in evening. Day dark & appearance of rain. Johnstone looking after his little boy who is very sick. He seems to be greatly affected with the child being so sick. It proves that there is a little love in some Niggars for their offspring. Wilhara tells me he wants some trade in the morning to buy copra.[46] Boy shot 6 pigeons. Jimy came over in the evening and wanted Johny to go to his father but would not let him.

Sunday 21st September

Thank God this is Sunday. No work today. We keep the day here although we are a long way out of civilisation. You cannot get the natives to knock of work on Sunday. Wilhara came for trade early this morning. I gave him 400. He is away in 'Buna' direction.

---

43 The *Helena* was a schooner of 126 tons, built in 1874, registered at Maryborough, and later lost at Inskip point, Queensland in July 1899 ('Encyclopaedia of Australian Shipwrecks and other Maritime Incidents', Yarram, Victoria: Oceans Enterprises, 2006, http://oceansl.customer.netspace.net.au/qld-main.html (Accessed June 2012)).

44 Unfortunately the diary record for the remainder of 17th September and for 18-19th September is missing, the page having fallen out of the diary.

45 Crossan's medical kit was very basic. St Jacob's oil was a patent liniment to relieve muscular aches. Salt pitre or petre was ingested to relieve various ills including fevers. Castor oil was used for stomach problems, especially constipation. Laudanum was a sedative consisting of tincture of opium, and was used for a range of complaints, to relieve pain and for coughs (see footnote to 6th January). While Crossan administers 'medicine' for fevers, we are not told that it was quinine.

46 In Solomon Islands sticks of tobacco were the normal currency for barter transactions of all kinds. The exchange rate of the early 1880s was generally 1 stick of tobacco per 10 coconuts (Bennett, *Wealth of the Solomons*, 53). Each coconut, when split and smoke-dried to copra, yielded 20 half-shells, and these were usually sold by Solomon Islanders as a 'string', i.e. they were strung together on a cord of sennit. Ten 'strings' constituted a 'bunch'.

[*Marginal note:*] Gave 400 trade. Return 80 50 12 [*= sub-subtotal of*] 148 49 45 [*= subtotal of*] 242 147 [*= total of*] 389 [*strings of copra?*]. 10 tob short.[47]

Darracks back very bad. One Medicin native gave him some medicin, looked like flour.[48] Rubbed it on his back but did not make much impression or give him any releifs. They make it out of some grass that grows in the bush. He is going to let me into the secret how to make it. It may be of some value. Day very dull and all appearance of rain. Set down some cocoanut yeast this evng. to see how it will turn out in bread baking.[49] Some improvement is wanted as we are eating regular rib stickler, which will no doubt fatten us in time.

Williara came back abt 4 p.m. with 1500 copra,[50] get more on Tuesday week. Had good dinner 'stewed pigeons'. Darracks back a little better, took some castor oil, had bath in evening. No appearance of Johnstone. Our boy Johny lef us this morning. Evening fine. Some men from the upper village here.

Monday 22ⁿᵈ Sept 85

No work today. Darrack's back still very bad consequently I can do nothing to the boat myself. Having a general squaring day in the House doing little odd

---

47 'Gave 400 trade' in this marginal note must refer to 400 sticks of tobacco for Wilhara to use for purchasing copra. The list of numbers probably refers to the number of strings of copra that Wilhara supplied in exchange ('Return') for the 400 sticks of tobacco. The total is 389, so that Wilhara is still '10 tob short' (actually eleven). It appears that copra is being calculated by Crossan according to its equivalent value in stick tobacco, showing that tobacco was, in effect, the unit of currency.

48 This 'medicin' was probably quick-lime. On Uki Island Guppy noted that 'chunam' or burnt lime was 'one of the domestic remedies employed in sickness, being rubbed into the skin of the patient by his friends. The chunam of some men is more efficacious than that of others' (Guppy, *The Solomon Islands and their Natives*, 163).

49 On a separate page in the notebook used for the diary is the following recipe, which we interpret as showing how Crossan used fresh coconut water to produce a fermentation based on wild yeasts: '7 cocoanuts, 1 tablespoonfull sugar, 4 tablespoonfull Flour. In bottle'. On this page is also a recipe which shows how Crossan used his yeast mixture as a starter, adding it to flour, sugar and warm water to make what bakers call a 'sponge', which is a mixture in which the yeast cells are encouraged to multiply:

'1 tablespoonful Vinigar
1 tablespoonful Sugar
4 tablespoonful Flour
Yeast
Mix with warm water
Let set for 4 hours'.

This sponge would have contained too little flour to make actual bread, but when it was bubbling with gas Crossan would have mixed in extra flour and then shaped his loaves. On the same page of the notebook is a note saying 'Let your Bread set for 8 hours', which perhaps was the period of final rising before the loaves were put into the oven (Prof. Helen Leach, University of Otago, personal communication, 2011).

50 Williara is presumably the same local trader as the Wilhara to whom Crossan had supplied 400 tobacco copra earlier that day. The '1500 copra' from Buna probably means '150 strings of copra', each string consisting of 20 half shells derived from 10 coconuts. The marginal note shows '148' as a sub-total, which is close enough to the figure of 1500 (i.e. 150 strings) in the diary entry. It is not clear if Wilhara is an employee of Crossan or a freelance contractor, but probably the latter. If so then he was either paying his Buna producers less for their copra than the 'official' exchange rate (one tobacco stick per string), or perhaps he was making his profit on sales of other trade goods for which the 'price' was more negotiable.

jobs. Shot a dog last night, [*illegible*] came along to see what was the matter & approved of me shooting the animal for stealing. Wether he ment it or not I do not know, he cut the teeth out of his head as it is their money here & is valuable.[51] Dog is a luxury. Similar to a Bush Native, they are both dog eaters & man eaters all over this island. For some cause or other they burried this one, at our request. One native in the house today was very bad with the Veneral disorder & ultimately it will finish him.[52] I was talking to the Medicin Man of the village. He says he will cure him if he gets paid. The Medicin Boy says he is a missionary, & I told him the missionary does anything of that sort for love of their fellow beings. He no savee it that way, he wants M.D., takes after European Doctory. Had a little rifle practice this afternoon. Day warm and showry. Johnstones Boy not expected to live. He will not leave the house till their boy is better or dead. Making a little copra out of our own trees.

Tuesday 23rd [September] 1885

Rose early & started to build boat. Wilhara woke us in the morning to let us know that Johnstone's boy had died in the night. They sent over a Labor Box[53]

---

51 Dog's teeth on Makira were counted in units of four, and they were regarded as more valuable than bats' teeth (Moira White, 'The material culture of Makira', in Atholl Anderson et al., eds. *Vastly Ingenious* (Dunedin: Otago University Press, 2007)). According to Codrington (*The Melanesians*, 325), on Makira only the dog's teeth situated immediately behind the canines had value, and to be worth much these had to be very white and sound. On Nggela one dog's tooth was equal in value to five porpoise teeth, but on Makira island one dog's tooth was worth one or two porpoise teeth depending on quality. European traders could exploit these differences. Bennett (*Wealth of the Solomons*, 84) describes how in 1887 the trader Jack Cooper found that the people on Nggela would exchange 50 copra (worth 5 sticks of tobacco) for one 'eye tooth' of a dog. Cooper knew that Uki islanders and Makira bush people had dog teeth, but they were reluctant to part with them unless in exchange they could obtain the more prized porpoise teeth. He therefore travelled to Makira Harbour where people craved tobacco. 'For 1 stick of twist tobacco he exchanged 4 porpoise teeth that at Uki bought him 2 dog teeth and were then traded to the Nggela people for 100 coconuts'. In this way 1 stick of tobacco traded at Makira (worth 10 copra) had been turned into 100 copra from Nggela.

52 'Veneral disease' could refer to either gonorrhoea or syphilis, both introduced diseases. However, the symptoms of syphilis could also be confused with yaws, an endemic disease caused by an organism closely related to that causing syphilis. Yaws was common in Makira and throughout Solomon Islands, and previous infection is thought to induce immunity to syphilis (Peter Pirie, 'The effects of treponematosis and gonorrhoea on the populations of the Pacific Islands', *Human Biology in Oceania* 1(3), 1972). However, there is no doubt that, as well as gonorrhoea, syphilis was present in Solomon Islands. Codrington (*The Melanesians*, 12) states that 'within my own recollection [i.e. post-1871] syphilis, or the venereal disease which was taken for it, was unknown in the islands visited by the Melanesian Mission, except at San Cristoval, where alone intercourse with whalers and traders had been considerable. It has lately become widely known, and it is certain that it has been brought back by returned 'labourers', male and female'. Woodford (*A Naturalist among the Head-Hunters*, 35) asserts that 'such cases [of sexually-transmitted disease], of course, are more common upon those islands where the unbridled and promiscuous licentiousness of the natives inhabitants renders it a matter of surprise that they are not more universal than they actually are'. Almost certainly Makira Island would have been included in the places renowned for 'licentiousness' (Bennett, *Wealth of the Solomons*, 29; Journal of Charles Hunter on *Southern Cross*, 23 May 1877, http://anglicanhistory.org/oceania/brown1877/ (Accessed December 2011)). Philp writing in 1912 quotes missionary opinion to the effect that on Makira female sterility (an effect of sexually transmitted disease) had contributed greatly to the depopulation of the island (Herr and Rood, *A Solomons Sojourn*, 141).

53 'Labor Box' refers to the trade box, which was typically a pine chest measuring 36 inches by 18 inches with a lockable lid. Each man returning from plantation labour in Fiji or Queensland would aim to bring home at least one box filled with his possessions (Adrian Graves, 'Truck and gifts: Melanesian immigrants and the trade box system in colonial Queensland', *Past and Present* 101, 1983, 88). The labour recruiter John

to make a coffin. We spent about 2 hours in arranging it the best way we could, lined it with white callico & outside with print, made it quite respectable for the corpse. I went over and they were crying & whining like cats & dogs, sickening to hear. 20 of the natives went to the bush for yams and taro to have a feast, after the growling is all over. When one lot is tired another starts, tonight it would frighten the devil the noise they make. Day warm and close accompanied with showers. Sea very calm. Saw a good few sharks out in the smooth water. Had good bath. But the cooking is our trouble, work and then cook your own food is what I do not care about, the natives are such a dirty lot of devils you can trust them to do nothing clean. One old man today made Darrack sick. He had the worst leg that is possible to conceive on a Human Being.[54] We sent him away. It is doctors they want down here not missionaries for in the course of a few years if things go on as they are they will be no more natives to instruct in the Bible & it is a great pity as they are a fair class of people.

Wednesday 24th Sept 85

Rose as usual, day showry and warm. Worked hard on boat & made good progress. Sandy came over with 300 copra, squared tob a/c.[55] He had some words with one of the men here, they say he chetted the Helena out of tobacco.[56] I thought they were going to have a fight. Gave him a little for trade. Steve's cutter sighted about 12 a.m. anchored a little above us, Jamie Niccol in charge.[57] Came ashore and had tea with us, looks very well, abt 8 tons copra on board 3 weeks out, very bad weather. Lef abt 12 p.m. for the cutter. It is more than likely that the boys here will have someone killed over this death.[58] This is to satisfy the devil they say. If a white man is speared, the spear is scraped & the scrapings are valuable & worth so much of their money.[59] Went to bed late sat up and baked bread.

Cromar (*Jock of the Islands*, 117) says that in each trade box, 'besides odds and ends, every boy had tobacco, pipes, matches and calico, and some also had butcher's knives and small axes'. After 1884 all trade boxes were inspected on board ship to make sure no firearms or ammunition had been included.

54 This could be a reference to the symptoms of filariasis, yaws or tropical ulcers. Crossan's remark indicates that the decline in numbers of the indigenous population was becoming obvious.

55 'Squared tob a/c' appears to mean that Crossan calculated the balance in the copra-tobacco exchanges that had taken place between himself and his agent Sandy. When Crossan then says 'gave him a little for trade' it implies that Sandy had been advanced further tobacco so that he could obtain more copra for Crossan.

56 Sandy is angry with a Hada man who, he says, 'chetted' (cheated) the *Helena* in a copra/tobacco exchange. Local traders like Sandy depended on maintaining relations of trust with visiting ships, which might avoid places where they had been 'cheated' on a previous visit.

57 James Nicol worked for Stephens (WPHC 33/86, WPA). 'Steve' is probably the trader John Stephens (see footnotes for 6th and 11th September).

58 'This death' refers to the death of Johnstone's son, which would have been attributed to sorcery.

59 Supernatural powers were evidently attributed to the scrapings, which may have induced sepsis or tetanus in the next victim quite apart from the wound inflicted by the spear.

Thursday 25th Sept 85

Rose very late, quite tired. Darrack working at boat. I am cooking & cleaning up the house, & getting the copra cut up. Day is warm & dull. I made a grand plum duff today, got it in the boiler but could not get it out, eats well. Johnstone sent us a present of a good big Rooster this morning. They are all preparing get wood yams taro coconuts pigs & fowls for the big feed tomorrow. The only thing they want to complete it is a dead bushman to eat & they would be set up. Still howling & crying. Some of the natives told me today they are going to keep it up for two moons. Steve's cutter left this morning abt 9 a.m. for Buna. Wilhara has just told me that Johnstone is not going to bury the child outside. He is going to keep it in a box in the house.[60] I will try to persuade him to bury the child outside. It is something not very nice to contemplate, having a corpse in the house. They have eat nothing since the death, so by this, they must take it very much to heart. Wilhara says Johnstone has got to cry for one moon yet some of the natives finish their cry tomorrow, & go home to work.

5 Buna men came in canoe today to pay their respects to the dead I suppose. One of them an ill looking cannbal brute with a ring through his nose, has been bechdemer fishing on the Indispensables.[61] He is a knowing Josser.[62]

The M.S. S. Cross Southern Cross has been down with Labor.[63] Made a good trip.

When the natives put their Medicine on your back they cross good & pray to the devil, it is what they call Chemaning.[64] Went to bed early, we keep the [*illegible*] here. But I do not know if it will turn out true or not. Early to bed & early to rise makes a man healthy & wise.

Friday 26th September 1885

Started work at boat early. Made splendid progress, finished all boarding up on sides. Men went out to catch fish, caught 270 beautiful eating fish, & sent some to us. Queen of Buna visited us today, gave her a little tobacco. Johnstone

---

60 The bodies of children were often kept or buried inside a dwelling house (Fox, *The Threshold of the Pacific*, 227-228). This seems to have been the custom in the general region. Ivens, the missionary ethnologist, reports that on the neighbouring island of Maramasike (Little Mala) 'A loved child is sometimes buried in the dwelling house... The body might also be tied to the pillar or placed in a large wooden bowl, or even in later days in the large wooden box which labourers brought back from Queensland' (Walter Ivens, *Melanesians of the South-East Solomons*, London: Kegan Paul, Trench, Trubner & Co., 1927, 213-4).

61 The Indispensable Reefs lie 50 km south of Rennell Island. The reported 'bechdemer fishing' refers to the diving, collecting and processing of holothurians (sea slugs, sea cucumbers or bêche-de-mer) to produce a dried product for the China trade.

62 A 'josser' is a slang term for a foolish or obnoxious person, and was used in the 19th century to describe a simpleton, a codger, a fop or a parasite (*Oxford English Dictionary*, http://www.oed.com/view/Entry/101694?redirectedFrom=Josser#eid (Accessed Aug. 2012).

63 *Southern Cross* was the headquarters ship of the Melanesian Mission, but Crossan is wrong to imply that this ship was also involved in the labour trade. It is possible that the mission ship was returning to their homes labourers who had been put ashore outside their own territory, for them a very dangerous situation.

64 When he writes 'what they call chemaning' Crossan means 'what they call chunaming', in other words applying *chunam* or quicklime as a medicinal remedy (see footnote to 21st September).

came over in the morning, gave him a glass of rum & some bread & biscuits, he seems very down hearted over the death. Gave us permission to shoot the child's fowls.[65] We cannot complain about the food here as we get plenty of change. Day warm and fine. Big feast today. Had bath in evening, had good dinner & retired for the night.

Saturday 27th [September] 85

Rose 6.00 a.m., prepared breakfast, sent boy to shoot pigeons, returned with 5. Day very hot. Put all copra out in the morning to dry. Men finished copra house, had it all thoroughly dried & stored it up. Buna men gave us assistance, looked up trade for Buna to send away tomorrow by canoe. Johnstone came this morning & had a good feed of beef & duff. He said it was grand. When talking about the death of his boy, the old man burst out in tears. I was really sorry for him. He has got the crown of his hair cut out in half moon shape. This is mourning in commemoration for the dead. All the men went to bush to procure cocoanuts for another big feast tomorrow. He brought a chain to fix up our door properly, so as when we went out we could lock it as no one could get in. He is really very kind & considerate towards us & in return we give him anything he asks. He appears to study our welfare as much as we do ourselves. Baked good bread today for a wonder (accidentally). Buna men going home tomorrow. No work at boat today. Men out getting wood suitable for her timbers. Retired early.

Sunday 28th Sept 85

No work this day. 'Opel Oh' which are thankfull for.[66] Buna people left today. Johnstone's wife's new canoe out catching fish. It is only allowed to catch one at a time being new. After it is seasoned to the fishing, then they can catch as many as they like in it. Day warm. Cutter in sight, steering for Uigi. Wilhara going to take trade to buy copra tomorrow. Retired early.

Monday 29th Sept 85

Rose early. Wilhara went to 'Laehow' with trade & returned 2,300.[67] Johnstone giving a hand in cutting timber for the boat. Made fair progress. Day warm & close. Rain fell in afternoon. Had good dinner. Darrack went out in canoe yesterday and got a capsize. He say he never knew anything go over so quick in his life.[68] First adventure and no doubt the last. Retired early.

---

65 In many Melanesian societies a person's property was destroyed after his death.
66 'Opel Oh' is Crossan's rendering of the cry 'Bell-Oh' that was used to signal rest periods on the Queensland plantations.
67 The village of 'Laehow' is the place that Crossan later spells Lohu, today called Rohu or Rohurua in Maro'u Bay. 'Lohu' was described by Captain Sorenson as 'about four miles west of Hadda Bay', with 'west' an obvious mistake for 'north' (Seizure for piracy, *The Brisbane Courier*, 28 December 1885, 5). The '2,300' that Wilhara returned with from Lohu must refer to the number of dried coconuts that he purchased there, equivalent to 230 strings of copra and worth about 230 sticks of tobacco.
68 Small outrigger and dugout canoes were both in use on Makira, as well as larger fishing canoes and war canoes. Joseph Atkin remarked in 1869 '[t]he San Christoval canoes are models of lightness and beauty; and

Tuesday 30th Sept 85

Rose early, started boat first thing. Darrack got all timbers cut & gummed ready. Gave her the first coat of paint inside. Men cutting up copra. Day warm. All the villagers in bush planting yam's.[69] The Dog Rover among the natives very much. They say he is half Dog and half Man. We put it on a lot with the natives such as whispering in his ear. They are all fond of him and at the same time very frightened in case they displease him. They fancy if they offend him he will eat them.

Wednesday October 1st 85

Rose early. Johnstone lit fire. Boy went out and caught some very nice mullet.[70] They are dabsters at spearing fish,[71] they could strike the eye of a mosquito at 40 yds with comfort. Went & procured knees & timbers for boat. Darrack hard at work cutting them for same. It is remarkably hard work getting timbers out of the bush. Johnstone is a great assistance when he sticks at work. The most disquieting part of the opera is cooking your own food after you have done a days work. Darrack says that a man without a woman is an ass. It proves itself here. Day warm, slight shower no wind.

Thursday Oct 2nd 85

Started to work at boat early. Morning fine. Cut out sail & commenced to make it. Schooner in sight abt 2 p.m., think John Hunt from Fiji.[72] Johnstone hard at work. Got a lot of fine mackerill & 2 pigeons. Very anxious to get finished with boat so as we can get in some copra. Retired late. Baking bread in evening.

Friday 3rd Oct 85

Johnstone & Darrack hard at work at boat. Made good progress today. Worked at sail all day. Heavy showers fell which freshens things up a bit. Men all in bush planting yams.

---

ours, with a crew of boys, went easier and faster than a whaleboat; but, unfortunately, she was very wet, being both leaky and shipping a great deal of water from the head sea' (letter quoted by J.J. Halcombe, *Mission Life: An Illustrated Magazine of Home and Foreign Church Work*, London: W. Wells Gardner, 1872, 140).

69 Yen found that in the early 1970s that on Makira island generally there was little cultivation of inland areas, even in seemingly favourable and accessible valleys, but he pointed out that 'much of the vegetation inland is secondary and could well indicate former cultivation … inland agriculture was practiced by coastal dwellers with the use of a field house for temporary sojourns' (Yen, 'Agricultural history and prehistory in the Solomon Islands', 63).

70 Possibly grey or flathead mullet, *Mugil cephalus*, a common fish species eaten in New Zealand (Maori *kanae*) as well as the Pacific Islands.

71 A 'dabster' is a slang word meaning 'expert' (*Oxford English Dictionary*. http://www.oed.com/view/Entry/46776?redirectedFrom=dabster#eid

72 Several vessels from Fiji were seeking to recruit Solomon Islands labour at this time (Corris, *Passage, Port and Plantation*, 43). 'John Hunt' is possibly Mr John Linn Hunt, son of a planter from Kandy, Ceylon, who arrived in Suva, Fiji, in 1885 and worked for the Rewa Sugar Company at Koronivia (*Cyclopedia of Fiji*, Sydney: The Cyclopaedia Company of Fiji, 1907, 238).

Saturday 4th Oct 85

Darrack & Johnstone hard at work on the boat, made good progress. Finished sail in the evening. Brigantine Lavina from Brisbane.[73] Labor. Hove in sight abt 2 p.m., landed 2 returns for Johnstone. One very sick had to be carried ashore. Went down. Appeared to be a very snooty G.A. & had little to say to him. Anchored in Hada Bay. Day warm, fresh breeze blowing. Wyloo gave us a hand in House.[74] Boat went to Lohu for copra, returned in evening with very little. Sandy gave us a visit in the afternoon. Gave him 4 Jews Harps.[75] Retired early.

Sunday 5th [October]

No work this day, devote the day to procuring good dinner. Lavina's boat came ashore with 5 Lohu returns. They are going to Lohu in Johnstone's boat in the morning. The Mackay returns speak very bad of Macky in respect to food and work. Prefer Fiji. Strong SSE breeze blowing. G.A. of Lavina was kind enough to bring us some Queensland papers ashore, so I must have formed a wrong opinion of him yesterday. Capt Williams in charge from Maryborough, intend leaving tomorrow. Lef Sept 10th had quick passage to here. Retired early.

Monday October 6th 1885

Started work at Boat, made good progress. Natives sent up for lend of oars, & I would not give them. Johnstone gave us a hand all day. In the afternoon he got the huff at something I said to him. He left of work & spoke to Darrack saying that I had said something about his sister. He says, he finish now, no work any more. I cannot think of what I said to the old fellow that he should take such offence as this. He says, suppose Boy here talk like that to me, he kill him quick.[76] It is just this with these Niggers. You don't know when you have them or not. He has been made a little to much of. However I will keep my eyes open. Day warm, fresh breeze blowing.

---

73 Probably the *Lavinia* (62 tons), a trading ship which in 1872-73 had landed in Sydney coconut oil, coconuts, copra, tortoise shell and sulphur from Solomon Islands, and in 1873 was involved in a violent confrontation on Nggela in which six Europeans and two Solomon Islanders were killed (Bennett, *Wealth of the Solomons*, 364, 390). Members of a boat's crew from *Lavinia* were killed on Epi, New Hebrides, in 1883, after an attack that was probably in retaliation for the deaths in Queensland of labour recruited from Epi (Deryck Scarr, *Fragments of Empire. A History of the Western Pacific High Commission 1877-1914* (Canberra: Australian National University Press, 1968), 172).
74 Wyloo's name is mentioned twice more in the next few days, but he then disappears from the record, unless Wyloo is the same person as 'Lo' who was drying Crossan's copra on 29th January.
75 The jew's harp, also called jaw, mouth or juice harp, is a musical instrument with a flexible tongue or reed attached to a frame, placed in the performer's mouth and plucked with a finger to produce a note. The indigenous types found in Island Melanesia were made of bamboo. Traded metal types of jew's harp were in high demand in both Polynesia and Melanesia in the nineteenth century (Mervyn McLean, *Weavers of Song: Polynesian Music and Dance*, Auckland: Auckland University Press, 1999, 356, 358).
76 Codrington (*The Melanesians*, 12) writes 'Speaking generally, it may be said that to a Melanesian man all women, of his own generation at least, are either sisters or wives.... The women who may be his wives by marriage, and those who cannot possibly be so, stand in a widely different relation to him... Intercourse

Tuesday Oct 7th 1885

Started at Boat, made good progress. Tomorrow expect to finish. Day fine fresh breeze blowing. Men out catching Bonito, caught 20. Johnstone came over in afternoon to show photo of his boy that is in Sydney.[77] Would not speak to me, not get over his huff yet. Wyloo gave us hand cooking. Retired early.

Wednesday 8 Oct

Started boat, made good progress. Johnstone caught some fish in morning, in a little better humour today, spoke to me. He seems very anxious to get the Boat finished. Wyloo looking after house all day. Day warm, strong trade breeze blowing, hard day's work. Retired early.

Thursday 9 Oct 85

Started at Boat, made good progress. Lowered her of blocks, to put out & paint. In morning Johnstone gave us a hand, in good humour today. Gave us an explanation that talking about sisters is tambooed. Darrack very bad with a kind of prickly itch, cant sleep.[78] Day warm, wind W. by S. Buried return man this morning.[79] The natives are immensely pleased with the boat. Retired early.

Friday 10th Oct 85

Got boat out, gave her a coat of paint outside. Day warm with nice breeze blowing. Darrack's leg very bad, swollen up. Retired early.

Saturday 11th Oct 85

Started & painted Boat inside. Day warm & pleasant wind W. by S. Johnstone gave us a hand all day, very good just now, can hardly do enough to please us. Darrack very bad, unable to work. Men away to have a big feed over the last dead man. Men all busy planting yams. Retired early.

---

within the limit which restrains from marriage, where two members of the same division are concerned, is a crime, is incest. In Florida [Nggela] in old times the man would have been killed, and the woman made a harlot. Now that the severity of ancient manners is relaxed, money and pigs can condone the offence...' Fox states that in Arosi '[a] man calls a woman of his own generation his sister'. He shows that in the case of actual brothers and sisters, and also cross-cousins, there are severe restrictions on social intercourse let alone marriage (Charles Fox, *The Threshold of the Pacific: an Account of the Social Organisation, Magic and Religion of the People of San Cristoval in the Solomon Islands* (London: Kegan Paul, Trench, Trubner, 1924), 23, 28). Possibly Johnstone's 'sister' was simply a female relative, possibly a cousin, with whom a sexual relationship was, for him, utterly unthinkable, literally beyond a joke.

77 Clearly one of Johnstone's close kin, a son or nephew, now lived in New South Wales and had managed to send him back a photograph. It is evidence of a remarkably modern transaction between two contrasted societies, and helps to explain Johnstone's ease and effectiveness in the role of go-between.

78 Almost certainly this was a case of prickly heat or *miliaria rubra*, a blockage of sweat glands and common in hot humid climates especially if clothing is worn.

79 The man referred to must be the returned labourer who landed from *Lavinia* on 4th October, 'very sick [and] had to be carried ashore'.

Sunday 12th Oct 85

Day of Rest. Passed the day reading & talking to the natives, house pretty much full all day.[80] Johnstone gave me a hand cleaning up the house. He is brick to work when he takes it into his head. Day warm, heavy showers fell in afternoon. Retired early.

Monday 13th October 1885

Scraped & oiled oars, launched Boat in water and went for a pull. Johnstone very much pleased with the Boat. Went to Suedangai's & got some copra.[81] Shouted for all the Boys in morning going to Buna. Had my first exploit in canoe today. Went all very well for a while, by got a little to venturesome,[82] result git a dip in the Briney. The natives did laugh. Took great care that I could always see the bottom, they don't catch me in deep water. Johnstone let us into a wrinkle[83] in reference to milk for our tea, it is equal to the best cream. Retired early.

Tuesday 14th October

Rose early, went to Buna, got copra.[84] Day very wet, got home late.

Wednesday 15 [October]

Working getting things squared up in the house. Baked bread & washed clothes, neither jobs do I like. Intend going to Morrow Bay[85] tomorrow morning to procure cocoanuts. Worked at sail in evening. Darrack a little better.

Thursday 16th October 85

Rose early, went to Morrow Bay. Day fine in morning but rained heavy in afternoon. Got about 3,000 nuts.[86] Got home at 9 p.m. 3 bushmen came down to House. Darrack much better.

---

80 This comment suggests that Crossan was already proficient in Tok Pisin or Pidgin English, and had developed sufficient trust in the Hada Bay people to allow them to come inside his house.
81 Suedangai is probably the same man who elsewhere is called Seudangi (20th October and 6th December), Swea (21st October), Sewa (26th October), Sewedanga (1st December), Seua (13th January), and Seudangai (27th January). He was a local trader based at Lunichena (probably Rumahui) about 8 km south of Hada Bay, not too far away and therefore very suitable for the maiden voyage of the new cutter.
82 The phrase 'by got a little to venturesome' includes both Pidgin and bad spelling, and should properly read 'by-and-by I got a little too venturesome', the word 'by' indicating 'later on' in Pidgin.
83 An informal meaning of 'wrinkle' is an ingenious trick or device, or a clever innovation (Random House Dictionary).
84 This entry shows that the new sailing boat was immediately put to use, and it enabled Crossan to make a 10 km journey to Ubuna and return with cargo the same day.
85 'Morrow bay' is Maro'u Bay, which Crossan would have sailed past on his way to Ubuna the previous day. The diary entry as written seems to imply that Crossan simply helped himself to the nuts, but this trip no doubt took place with the approval and possibly the participation of the local chief or big-man (i.e. Johnstone and/or the 'King of Buna').
86 Depending on their size, 3000 coconuts would be sufficient to make between 0.3 and 0.9 ton of copra. At the time copra was worth to the trader between £7 and £8 per ton (Bennett, *Wealth of the Solomons*, 53).

Friday 17th Oct 85

Cleaned oars. Darrack fixed up Boat & sail. Day wet & miserable. Jimey installed as cook but I do not expect him to keep at it long.

Saturday 18th Oct 85

Rose early. Paint oars & done odd jobs about House & Boat. Men broke copra to smoke. Johnstone told us of another man from Gaudalcanel that he killed & eat. He was walking abt all day with a pair of spectacles, got capsized in his canoe, bringing wood. Retired early.

Sunday Oct 19 85

Rose early. Glencairn[87] in sight. Went of on board, all well, took of yams, cocoanuts fish &etc. Baker[88] came ashore, to stay till ship come back from 'Malata'.[89] Left her abt 2 p.m. for 'Malata' to land 3 boys. Expect her back in 3 days. Retired early.[90]

---

87 The *Glencairn* was a trading and/or labour recruiting vessel based in Fiji, and on this occasion it seems to have had no licence to recruit labour but was able to take on copra as a return cargo, as occurred also on a later voyage (see footnote for 3rd September). In anticipation of this opportunity, Crossan and Baker collected together all the copra they could from the hinterland of the Hada Bay trading station.

88 Baker founded the company 'Baker, Crossen & Co.' of Fiji, and was the person who had originally purchased land at Hada Bay for the trading station (Bennett, *Wealth of the Solomons,* 378). Baker was on board *Glencairn* from August to December 1875, in a voyage that included also the New Hebrides.

89 'Malata' is the island of Malaita, an important source of recruits for the labour trade.

90 On a later and separate page of the notebook is the following note, probably written on this same day:

   '85 Oct 19th   Woman Buna
                      100 tob
                      20 matches
                      12 bead's
                      By 73 Copra
                      Jim Trader 2 rings'

The 'Woman Buna' seems to be Crossan's only local trader who is female, although 'girls' sold copra to him as individuals (see 5th December entry). The words 'By 73 Copra' must mean 'Buy [I bought from her] 73 strings of copra', while the list of tobacco, matches and beads is probably the amount of goods that Crossan gave to the woman of Ubuna as payment, or perhaps supplied to her on credit in expectation of further copra being forthcoming. 'Jim' was probably one of Crossan's already established 'traders'. No doubt there was another account book in which Crossan kept a full record of such transactions. If this interpretation is correct, then it is interesting to note that women as well as men were being used as agents in this way, and that the transactions were almost indistinguishable from classic Melanesian reciprocal exchange. In this case, it seems likely that the Ubuna woman's copra was exchanged for 100 sticks of tobacco, plus matches and beads, but at a generous rate of exchange that exceeded the usual price (100 rather than 73 sticks tobacco in exchange for 73 strings of copra) in the hope there would be a future 'gift' to Crossan of more copra. Alternatively Crossan 'bought' 73 copra at the normal price and then gave her more trade goods as either 'advance' (Crossan's concept) or 'gift' (probably the local interpretation).

4. Crossan's Hada Bay Diary

Monday 19 Oct 85[91]

Rose early, went to Buna & Tawatana.[92] Bought yams & copra. Baker went with me. Got back abt 6 p.m. Lunichuea men killed Bushman,[93] part of the corpse came here. Someone had to be killed owing to the Big Canoe being launched.[94] Retired early.

Tuesday 20 Oct

Worked in getting copra dried, and cut up. Went to Linichena in afternoon and got copra from Seudangi & Sandy. The corpse was cooked today. I was astonished when I came back & Darrack told me that some of the corpse was brought back cooked in the boat & the boys had a feed of it in front of the house. Our cook is away to get a feed of it at present, so much for canabalism. Sandy came over from Tawai tonight with copra.[95]

Wednesday 21st October 85

Went to Anutua[96] in morning. Called in at Linichena & got Swea & Sandy. Long pull down. Called in at Anutua & left trade with two men. The natives apparently are very knowing. Men had food their. Lef abt 4 p.m., got back to Lunichea & seen skull of man that was killed by Sandy. Got one small turtle. Sandy pointed out the place that he killed the man. He is a bit of a lion amongst the natives now. Bought some yam's. Got home abt 7 p.m.

---

91 By repeating the date, Crossan here corrects the error that he initiated on 6th September.
92 Tawatana is a village about 3 km east of Ubuna. Tawatana had been the home village of Stephen Taroaniara, the Anglican pastor who seemed destined to become the first Melanesian to be ordained as a priest but who was killed at Nukapu with Bishop Patteson in 1871 (Fox, *Lord of the Southern Isles*, 154).
93 'Lunichena' is the first of many references to a coastal village that is spelt in at least eight different ways in the diary (Lunichea, Linichona, Linichena, Linuchena, etc.). None of the Crossan spellings match any place shown on modern maps, but it seems to be located south of Hada Bay on the coast between Tawaraha and Harani'ia Point, possibly Rumahui.
94 This allegation is repeated on 2nd October and it sounds sensationalist, but is probably accurate. Codrington (*The Melanesians*, 297) writes: 'In the Eastern Solomons [Makira, Santa Anna, Santa Cruz, etc.], if no victim was met with in the first voyage of a new [war] canoe, the chief to whom the canoe belonged would privately arrange with some neighbouring chief to let him have one of his men, some friendless man probably, or a stranger, who would then be killed perhaps as he went out to look at a new canoe. It was thought a kind thing to come behind and strike him without warning.' Crossan's account also generally tallies with that of Ivens, who states that a new decorated overseas canoe, after going on tour to be shown off and to collect gifts, would return home where a man would be killed (Ivens, *Melanesians of the South-East Solomons*, 149-154).
95 Sandy's 'Tawai' was probably the village of Tawaraha, 3 km south of Hada Bay. For Crossan Tawaraha was the first stopover on his way south to Lunichea (Rumahui), about 7 km from Hada and the home base of Seudangi, another of Crossan's agents. 'Swea' who Crossan met in Lunichea the following day is probably the same man as Seudangi (see footnote for 13th October).
96 Anutua is Anuta (also called Ianuta or Yanuta), a small island in Makira Bay off the south coast adjacent to the mainland village of Onibia. Crossan does not give the name of his Anuta trader although he returned there on several occasions. The situation at Anuta may not have changed much when Joseph Dickinson visited the place thirty years later on a trading ship: 'The trading station here was again looked after by an old, returned Queenslander. His stock-in-trade consisted of stick tobacco, matches, clay pipes, knives, axes, beads, and Jews'-harps... Toby, the trader, was supplied with limited stock, as it was known that the natives often exercised extremely socialistic ideas at short notice; perhaps to appease some chief's sorrow or death or disappointment. No trading station enjoyed immunity when the policeman was up the next street' (J.H.C. Dickinson, *A Trader in the Savage Solomons* (London: H.F. & G. Witherby, 1927), 57-58).

Thursday 22nd Oct 85

Worked about House. Wrote a few letters & arranged up trade & Books. Johnstone working at copra. Sandy's big canoe away to Lunichena to demand money, about 30 boys in canoe. At every launch one man is killed & then they go round & demand trade & money.[97] Day wet & miserable. Retired early.

Friday 23rd Oct 85

Heavy rain during night cleared up in morning. Day fine. Fiddled about the house all day. Johnstone caught some mackerill in evening.

Johnstone was telling me that if a woman eats pork or fish & planted yams they would be no good. After eating pork or fish they stay in the house for 4 days. He says he has known plenty of instances where this has occurred. Jim the cook is over at the Boys house, praying to the devil. I intend going to see them. Retired early.

Saturday 24 Oct 85

Cut up copra and made table. Darrack made a rustic chair. Worked abt doing odd work. Lunichena war canoe came in sight about 3 p.m. I went down on the beech & one of the men came ashore & I paid him tob paper & matches. It is the customary thing for all the villages to pay something on all occasions like this. It will raise me in their estimation abt 2 pieces of pork better.

Fore & Aft Schooner hove in sight abt 6.30 p.m. Went out to meet her with 6 boys. Got near but the fog, wind & rain came and so heavy that we lost sight of her, island and all. We picked up the house light when of Hada Bay. Got home wet. So much for running after vessels in the dark, no more for me. Day wet & misearable. Expect Glencairn I expect tomorrow. Retired early.

Sunday 25th Oct 85

No work today, wet & miserable. Johnstone went out & caught a very peculiar fish, cured the head of it. Sandy came over, was a little dissappointed at the price of the copra. Thought it was 1,000 for 20/-.[98] Had a little rifle practice, retired early.

---

97 This entry refers to human sacrifice as well as the ritualised gifts that were had to be made when an important war canoe was newly launched. A large clinker-built war canoe that Codrington (*The Melanesians*, 294) saw being built at Ha'ani (Fagani) was 45 feet long and could carry 90 men. In Crossan's account 'money' almost certainly means strings of shell money, the basis for much gift exchange on Makira Island (see entry for 22nd December). The reference to 'trade' suggests that traded goods like tobacco had already been incorporated into the rituals surrounding canoe building and, no doubt, into other 'traditional' transactions. On 24th October Crossan himself 'paid' the visiting Lunichena war canoe with a gift of tobacco, paper for cigarette making and matches.

98 Sandy was hoping to receive 20 shillings (or £1) for 1,000 copra, these half shells coming from 500 coconuts. The hoped-for price implies that one ton of copra, derived from about 7000 nuts, might be worth £14. Resident traders at this time could only gain a beach price of about £7 or £8 per ton (Bennett, *Wealth of the Solomons*, 53). This price suggests that Sandy did indeed have inflated expectations and had reason to be disappointed. Crossan does not tell us what he actually paid Sandy, but something less than 10/- per 1,000 copra would have been a realistic rate.

Monday 26 October 1885

Schooner not yet in sight. Getting a little concern abt her. Sewa's brother down from Bush this morning.[99] Filled copra in bags this afternoon. Johnstone out and caught some fine fish, salted them for ship. Baker Darrack & I out in canoes in afternoon. I got 2 tips over, amused the natives very much. Got word tonight that a Fiji Schooner's left a Boy belonging to here at Anutua.[100] Boy walked from there to Linichena today & will be here in the morning. Retired early.

Tuesday 27th [October] 85

No sign of ship yet. Fiji Returns came from Anutua this morning. One was working on the Rewa,[101] the other Boat's Crew with Mr Milne. It was the Albatross that landed them, Capt. Meredith in charge, Arrow G.A., 13 days from Suva. Johnstone out & caught some fish. Missed a No. 4 cartridge out of house, spoke to Johnstone abt it & the knife, he is going to see into it. Day wet & miserable. Played a game of cards in the evening. Retired early.

Wednesday 28th Oct 85

Rose early, made a cupboard. Day wet & miserable, expecting schooner. Retired early.

Thursday 29th Oct 85

Rose early. Got a false keel out for Boat. Schooner hove in sight abt 2 p.m. Filled up copra & went on board, got out our trade & came ashore.[102] All well. Retired early.

---

99   Sewa is probably the trader Suedangi from Lunichea (Rumahui) – see footnotes for 13th and 20th October.
100   By 1939 Heranigau on the mainland near Anuta Island, Rumahui (probably Lunichea) and Ha'ateia (Hada Bay) were connected by a 'road' that extended further north almost to Maro'u Bay (Green, 'A history of post-Spanish European contact in the Eastern District', 45). We can infer that footpaths between the various Arosi-speaking coastal villages were already present in 1885 when this particular journey was made by the returned labourer, who thereby avoided contact with bush communities and the associated risks of violence. Crossan's interest in this returned labourer is not that he was dropped at Anuta rather than Hada Bay (although this action was illegal). Because the returned man was from Fiji this raised the possibility that *Glencairn* was the ship involved. In fact the ship was the *Albatross*, as Crossan learnt the following day, which had landed five returns at Anuta on 24th October before sailing along the south coast. *Albatross* then left for Guadalcanal and other islands, before returning on 25th November to Cape Keibeck in north-east Makira to drop men from that area (G. Pilkington, Journal of *Glencairn*, No. 56, 1 August-8 December 1885, NAF).
101   Most of the sugar cane plantations in Fiji were in the Rewa delta. Before the arrival of indentured labour from India in 1879 Fiji planters were highly dependent on labour recruited from Solomon Islands and New Hebrides.
102   This schooner was the *Glencairn*, the ship that had landed Crossan, Baker and Darrack at Hada Bay two months before (see footnote for September 3rd). It returned to Hada Bay after dropping off returned labourers on Malaita.

Friday 30 Oct 85

Filled bags with copra & took off to schooner, took some trade of ship. Fitted up back door in afternoon. Boat, with Darrack & Pilkington,[103] went of to ship after tea. Baker stayed ashore. Day warm & fine. Retired early.

Saturday 31 Oct 85

Sent of boat to ship, sent letters by Darrack & Baker, put ballast in schr. Stayed there all day, came home in evening. Ned came ashore with me. Sorry at parting with Darrack.[104] Came of at 5 p.m., schooner put to sea. A few of the natives went through some antics at parting with Darrack. Retired early.

Sunday Nov 1st 85

Steves cutter[105] in sight, anchored & boat came ashore in evening. Johnstone away to Lohu, day warm & fine, worked abt house, no natives about. Retired early.

Monday 2nd Nov 85

Day warm & fine. Cutter put out to Marau.[106] Fresh breeze. Worked at keel of boat. Johnstone clearing away stones. Ned worked up the fire place in cookhouse. Retired early.

Tuesday 3rd Nov

Finished keel on boat, painted them. Johnstone falling bush. Day warm & fine. Retired early.

Wednesday 4 Nov 85

Painted boats & done odd work abt them. Johnstone clearing up stones. House full in the evening, listening to the natives. Retired early.

---

103 G. Pilkington was the Government Agent on *Glencairn*, and his journal of this voyage survived in the Fiji Immigration Department. It is now in Central Archives, Government of Fiji (G. Pilkington, Journal of *Glencairn*, No. 56, 1 August-8 December 1885, NAF; Scarr, *Fragments of Empire*, 344).

104 Darrack and Baker left on the *Glencairn* to go back to Fiji. It seems that 'Ned' (surname not recorded) replaced them at Hada Bay. Ned was Edward Griffiths, who left his position as able seaman on the ship to become a 'hut keeper' with Crossan (G. Pilkington, Journal of *Glencairn*, No. 56, 1 August-8 December 1885, NAF; *Suva Times*, 12 Dec. 1885, NAF). Thanks to Prof. Ian Campbell for finding this reference in the *Suva Times*.

105 This is probably the cutter that belonged to the Stephens trading station at Uki, a potential rival for buying the copra along this coast (see footnote for 'Tunin', 6th September).

106 'Marau', the destination of John Stephen's cutter, is ambiguous. Crossan may mean Maro'u Bay 10 km north of Hada Bay, or possibly Marau Sound in northeast Guadalcanal where traders had been living intermittently since about 1876 (Bennett, *Wealth of the Solomons*, 283). More likely it is Wawa Marau Island beyond Makira Harbour, which Steve's cutter visited again on 6th December.

Thursday 5 Nov 85

Finished Boats and put them out in the water. Johnstone & 3 Boys clearing rubbish round the house. Got some nice fish in the morning. Looked up trade for Buna & Wanga,[107] intend going there tomorrow if it is fine.

Friday 6 November 1885

Morning gloomy & looked like rain, deferred the trip to Wanga till tomorrow. New moon appears in the morning of the 7th.[108] Day turned out fine. Johnstone & Boys falling bush behind house. Start for Buna & Wanga in the morning, wet or dry. Retired abt 10 p.m.

Friday[109] 7th Nov 85

Day fine. Nothing of importance to note.

Saturday 8th Nov 85

Went to Buna, stayed there all night, made my boots a pillow, & passed a most miserable night.[110]

Sunday 9th Nov 1885

Started in morning for Heula, called in at Tawatana & got Labea & brother & then went to Heula.[111] Lef trade & both places got copra & yams from Buna & left some more trade there. Got home late.

---

107 'Wanga' probably refers to Wango Bay, 18 km east of Ubuna. Wango had been a base for the Melanesian Mission since 1869. The missionary in residence from 1880-1894 was Richard Comins, but Wango may have been without a resident missionary in 1885 as Comins was attempting that year to reopen the school at Sa'a in Malaita (Michael Blain, 'The Blain biographical directory of Anglican clergy in the Pacific', http://anglicanhistory.org.nz.blain_directory.pdf 2008). Wango was visited by J.E.Philp for copra trading in 1912-13, and was described by him as a 'snug anchorage' (Herr and Rood, *A Solomons Sojourn*, 40). Two days after Crossan declared his intention to visit Wango he postponed his planned trip, and he never journeyed as far eastwards during the whole of his seven months at Hada Bay. The coast at Wango was probably part of the trading area of John Stephens based in Uki Island, and a reluctance to encroach on his competitor's territory may have been the reason for Crossan deciding not to visit.
108 Crossan is planning the longer trips that were now feasible in his new sailing cutter, and he does so with an eye to the moon's phases, new on 6th, first quarter on 14th and full on 22nd November. Moonlight would be helpful in case of delay and the need to sail the boat at night.
109 By repeating the Friday Crossan departs again by one day from the correct calendar that he had been following since 19th October.
110 This is the first occasion that Crossan spent a night away from Hada Bay, and it signifies his growing confidence about his personal safety. It is not clear from the diary if he spent the night ashore or slept in his boat.
111 Heula is probably the village of Heuru, 5 km east of Tawatana. The Melanesian Mission priest Richard Comins established a school there in 1885, but Comins's area of responsibility was the whole of the South East Solomons so he was often absent from Heuru – as on this occasion when he was on Malaita. Lahea, a local trader based in Tawatana, is mentioned again on 22nd January.

Monday 10 Nov

Cut up copra & fixed up house, day fine, intend going to Morrow Bay for nuts in morning.

Tuesday 11 Nov 85

Went to Morroo Bay, fair wind down. Buna been there smoking nuts.[112] Pitched the tent & turned in with the Boys for the night. Wet.

Wednesday 12 Nov 85

Fine morning. Men all at work getting nuts. Johnstone put down a charge of *[symbol for dynamite]* & got 200 fish, fine feed for the men.[113] Left there abt 1 p.m., got home abt 6 p.m. Day fine, all well at home.

Thursday 13th November 1885

Broke up nuts to smoke copra. Johnstone got in some wood. Day showry. Nothing to note, retired early.

Friday 14th [November]

Johnstone smoking copra, Boys cutting up. Day warm & showry. Women making mats. 2 Bushmen came down, want trade to go into Bush but I object.[114] Retired early.

Saturday 15th [November]

Johnstone busy smoking copra, Boys busy cutting up. Mulhau man came down with oars today.[115] Showry, creek very much fuller.

Sunday 16th [November]

Boat went to Lohu to get Copra, came back with 350. Queensland Labor Brigantine anchored in Hada bay abt 12 p.m., full of Boys from Guadalcanar, Jack on board.[116] Sandy came from Luichena brought a little Copra. Day warm & fine, retired early.

---

112 Maro'u Bay appears to have been an uninhabited part of the coast with many stands of coconuts, and it was visited by Ubuna people as well as Hada Bay people, as on this occasion.

113 It was perhaps Johnstone's presence on this trip to Maro'u Bay that persuaded Crossan that it was safe to sleep ashore in the tent overnight, as well as legitimate to harvest the coconuts.

114 Crossan's refusal to allow trade items to be sent into the Bush (i.e. inland areas) signals his own distrust of bushmen, but he may also have been influenced by Johnstone. Coastal chiefs like Johnstone had no wish to give up the monopoly over trade with white men that they enjoyed. It was probably a major reason for the later abandonment of inland areas, as the declining bush populations moved to vacant coastal sites where they could gain direct access to the copra trade.

115 The place 'Mulhau' cannot now be identified, but the diary entry for 17th November suggests that it was a village not far inland from Hada Bay, within an area that had timber suitable for making oars.

116 Two days later Crossan discovered that this Queensland brigantine was the *Young Dick* from Maryborough. The identity of 'Jack' is unknown; it may be the same person as the trader Jack from Lehua (modern Rihu'a) near Makira Harbour (see entry for 3rd March).

Monday 17th [November]

Day fine & warm, Johnstone smoking Copra. Went up to Mulhau after dinner. Looked at the yam plantation it is a most tedious job yam planting.[117] Retired early. Sent trade by Kiellehea to Lohu.

Tuesday 18th Nov 85

Wilharra came down last night & told me it was the Young Dick[118] from Maryborough 120 Boys on board, 6 weeks out. Went up to Mulhau yesterday & had a look at the yam planting. Day warm. Johnstone away at the yam garden's. SW breeze blowing. Johnstone clearing scrub in the afternoon. Intend going to Mackeria[119] tomorrow night.

Wednesday 19 [November]

Day warm. Bussy cutting firewood in bush all day. Got trade ready to start to Anutua. Intend being away all night & go to Mackeria.[120]

Thursday 20th [November]

Got to Anutua abt 2 a.m. 4 boys came with me to Mackiria. Got there at day break. Left trade at 3 places. Strong breeze coming back, arrived home abt 7 p.m.

Friday 21st [November]

Cut up the copra I got from Anutua. Slept very sound last night. 1 Brigantine & 1 Fore & A schooner in sight.[121] Day warm & close, having a general loaf today.

Saturday 22nd [November]

Day warm & fine. No work & general loafing & no copra coming in.

---

117 Crossan's lack of enthusiasm for yam gardens is in contrast to Codrington's appreciation (*The Melanesians*, 303): 'A garden of yams carefully trained on reeds, kept absolutely clear from weeds, and beautiful in the leafage of the vines, is a fine sight indeed; gardens, in San Cristoval as an example, with the various plots within a common fence neatly marked and divided, shew the exact regard for individual rights'.
118 In the following year *Young Dick* was attacked twice in Malaita, first at Port Adam and later at Sinerango, in retaliation for the deaths of young men recruited for Queensland, the sons of important men of those places (Corris, *Passage, Port and Plantation*, 41).
119 'Mackere', 'Mackria' and 'Mackeria' are all versions of Makira Harbour.
120 There was a full moon on 22nd November 1885, making this all-night sailing trip feasible.
121 This ship proved to be the *Princess Louise* (Captain Sam Craig), which avoided calling at Hada Bay but two days later was trading on the north coast at Rohurua and Ubuna, places well within Crossan's territory.

Sunday 23rd Nov

Day warm & fine fresh breeze blowing. Johnstone away cutting wood for the verandah. Fired up one side of the Copra House, this is the first Sunday any work has been done. The natives take fits & starts at work & the only way to get anything done is to let them work when they are in the humor.

Monday 24th [November]

Day warm & fine. Johnstone & Boys fixing up verandah. 2 canoes from Lohu came this morning and told us that Sam Craig[122] had called there yesterday & took copra there & Buna, and then went on to Makira.[123] Mulhau Boys seen Man of War yesterday making for Ugi. Hauled up Boat.

Tuesday 25th [November]

Day warm & fine. Boys in Bush yam planting. No work.

Wednesday 26th [November]

Day warm & fine. Finished the verandah. One Boy brought back by Capt. Craig came here this morning (Manumua) and gave us the account of Capt Peter Sorenson,[124] his doings & carrying on at Sockatoo. The Ongu fish came in last night & there was a good few caught. The place was quite illuminated up with

---

122 Sam Craig was the man who helped Otto Ashe to expose the activities of the criminal and psychopathic pearl diver and trader Peter Sorenson (Hugh Laracy, 'Niels Peter Sorenson: the story of a criminal adventurer', *Journal of Pacific History* 35, 2000, 153). Nearly a year later the same Captain Craig of the *Princess Louise* was delivering to Sydney in October 1886 a cargo of 75 tons of copra, 2 tons of beche-de-mer, 1 ton of pearlshell, 3,000 coconuts and some coconut oil (Bennett, *Wealth of the Solomons*, 370). Later Sam Craig was instrumental in closing down the Hada Bay trading station. In 1891, while employed by the Sydney trading company Thomas Waterhouse, Craig was murdered at Makira Bay by an islander named Tom. This man wanted revenge on Craig after his experiences in Noumea, as one of a party of 20 recruits working in the mines, seven of whom died (Corris, *Passage, Port and Plantation*, 68).
123 Crossan is here recording the activities of a business rival who was trading from places that Crossan would have regarded as his own 'territory'. Sam Craig's opportunism demonstrates the growing competition at this time between rival traders. The agents at Lohu, Buna and Makira would normally have supplied Hada Bay with copra.
124 Corris (*Passage, Port and Plantation*, 102) summarises the career of Niels Peter Sorenson as follows: 'Sorenson had a long and turbulent career in the Pacific, and served eight years in Brisbane Gaol for robbery and assault under arms. He was a psychopath and a sadist, with no regard for the lives of others, Europeans and islanders alike... In 1884 Sorenson signed on as crew seven men from Makira who were encouraged to engage by 'Johnson', the chief of Hada Bay [i.e. Crossan's 'Johnstone']. Provoked by Sorenson's erratic and violent temper, the seven natives of San Cristoval and some other crew members deserted his ship *Douro* at Ulawa and made their way in the ship's boat to New Britain. Sorenson sailed to New Britain but the deserters refused to rejoin him and were supported in their stand by a German official. One man remained in New Britain, three took ship for Sydney aboard a trading vessel, and the other three made their way back to their homes after serving aboard ships of the Deutsche Handels-und Plantagen Gesselschaft der Südseeinseln and visiting Samoa'. Captain Sorenson himself arrived in Hada Bay a month later and provided Crossan with a rather different story (see entry and footnote for 14th December). 'Sockatoo' is probably Cockatoo Island near Santa Isabel, an island which Sorenson was later to claim as his own.

canoe lights. It is something similar to the Polo caught in Samoa. The natives knows to a day when the fish will appear, it only comes once a year, two moons before the big wind.[125]

Thursday 27th [November] 85

Day warm & fine. Bushmen down in Hada Bay with Copra, all the men from here away. There armed to the teeth, big talk today, no more fight. Brought home some turtle eggs, about 30, I put the most of them back in the sand again. Painted the water line of the Boat.

Friday 28th 1885 Nov

Day fine. Johnstone cutting posts for house at back. Sandy came here today, giving me as usual all the bad faults of the natives. Gave him some trade. All the Boys in bush yam planting.

Saturday 29th [November]

Day warm & fine, strong S.W. breeze blowing. Johnstone busy building house at back & putting up fences. Jim away giving John a hand at yam planting.

Sunday 30th [November]

Day wet & windy. Natives all in their houses. About 3 p.m. a very heavy shock of earthquake passed through the island, running E. and W. Rolled some big stones down. I ran out of the house. Some long time ago a big Tidal Wave visited the island & carried canoes, houses and everything up into the bush.[126]

---

125 The Samoan 'palolo' (not 'palo') is *Palola viridis*, an annelid worm of South Pacific reefs that burrows in the coral and swarms in large numbers once a year. Crossan had worked for McArthur & Co. in Samoa in 1884 and may have witnessed the palolo season in November of that year, as well as half-learning the Samoan name. Walter Ivens states that on Ulawa island 'The annelid *palolo viridis* … attains a length of six to eight inches, the colours being bright red, or bluish black, or light yellow. The day of swarming is the second night after the full moon in November… It is only in November that it is fit for eating and appears in swarms. During the rest of the year the annelid lives in the coral rocks' (Ivens, *Melanesians of the South-East Solomons*, 313). According to Fox (*Arosi Dictionary*, 550) the Arosi words for palolo are 'barenga', 'ogu' and 'oku', the last two words being very similar to Crossan's 'ongu'.
126 Earthquakes and associated tsunamis are frequent events in Makira, the island being part of a very active 350 km segment of the North Solomon Trench along a major plate tectonic boundary (Paul Mann and Asahiko Taira, 'Global tectonic significance of the Solomon Islands and Ontong Java convergence zone, *Tectonophysics* 389, 2004, 137-190). In October 1930 severe earthquakes followed by tsunamis destroyed 18 major villages and caused many landslides (R.Thompson and P. Pudsey-Dawson, 'The geology on Eastern San Christoval, 1955-56', *Memoir, Geological Survey of the British Solomon Islands* (London: Crown Agents, 1958), 91). It is possible that this reference by Crossan to 'a big tidal wave' refers to legends of an island called Teonimanu which is said to have disappeared after it was hit by several big waves: 'After the tsunami hit the island, the people left alive paddled their canoes or clung to anything that floated to try and reach nearby islands. Some reached the north coast of Makira, where, expecting conflict, they fled to the mountains but were later looked after by local people…' (Patrick Nunn et al., 'Geohazards revealed by myths in the Pacific', *South Pacific Studies* 27, 2006, 42).

Monday December 1st 1885

Dull and showry. Johnstone at work at back. Sewedanga[127] here for trade. They felt the earthquake very heavy at Lunichena. Johnstone told me some long time ago it was that bad that they could not walk abt & a great many houses all over the island fell down.

Tuesday 2nd [December]

Dull day. Johnstone working at house. Men yam planting. Cleared a few of the boys out of the domicile today which they did not seem to approve of.

Wednesday 3rd [December]

Day dull & showry. Boat away to Lunichena, brought back 900 copra. Johnstone busy at house. Tawatana & Buna men here today, brought some Beetle Nuts for their friends, like a ship to put in to get some books to read.[128] Island life is fairly nice, but a trifle monotonous.

Thursday 4th [December]

Day warm & fine. Tawatana men went away this morning. Gave them some trade & the small boat to work copra, very much pleased at getting the boat.[129] Johnstone working at house.

Friday 5th [December]

Day very fine & warm. Johnstone working at House. Mulhau Girls down with some copra.[130] Luatto & 3 men from Anutua, gave them some trade. Cutter in sight steering for Ugi. Schooner (labour) of Mackeria, recruiting. NNW wind blowing. Intend going to Mackeria in a day or two.

Saturday 6th December 1885

Day warm & fine. Steve's Cutter came to Tawai this morning took in copra, & then put out to Wawa.[131] Vessell in sight long way of to the W. Boat brought 1,500 copra from Lunichena this morning. Gave Seudangi more trade. This

---

127 'Sewedanga' is probably the same man as 'Suedangai' who was first mentioned on 13th October, and also 'Sewa' whose brother was mentioned on 26th October.
128 Betel nuts (*Areca catechu*) provide a mild narcotic and are often shared amongst friends, the nut being mixed with lime and chewed with the leaf of *Piper betel*.
129 Crossan is happy to act generously by lending his small whale boat to Tawatana, knowing that its main use would be to transport coconuts for copra that would ultimately be sold to him.
130 Mulhau is a village with close links to Hada Bay but located a short distance inland. This reference to 'Mulhau Girls' indicates that even at this early date women were not excluded from trading copra.
131 'Tawai' may be the village of Tawaraha just south of Hada Bay. The diary entry suggests another noteworthy occasion of 'poaching' by John Stephens of Uki into the trading territory now occupied by Baker and Crossan at Hada Bay. 'Wawa' is probably the island of Marau Wawa just south of Makira Harbour (Fox, *The Threshold of the Pacific*, 4). It is called Marau Island on modern maps.

afternoon I shot an eagle with the Snider 200 yds out on a rock.[132] As a shootist I am 10 cocoanuts in advance now of any other white man with the natives. Intend going to Mackeria tomorrow.

Sunday 7th Dec

Beautiful day, S. wind blowing, big Kiki on at the village in commemoration of the yams being finished.[133] Some strange natives put in their appearance this afternoon, Bushmen. If fair wind going to Mackeria tonight.

Monday 8th Dec 85

Went to Heula & got copra, also Tawatana & Buna. Stayed at Morrow Bay all night. Evening wet. Got altogether abt 7,000.[134]

Tuesday 9th Dec

Morning fine, started for home abt 10 a.m., fair breeze. Boys cutting copra at Morrow Bay. Got home abt 3 p.m. Just heard of another outrage committed in the Bush. The King came down to Anutua to sell copra to one of my traders & on his way home was surprised & killed by another mob of bushmen. The natives here seem to be very jublaint over the affair, they tell me that he was a terror to most of the boys.[135]

---

132 Probably the Solomon Sea-Eagle *Haliaeetus sanfordi*, an endemic species most frequently encountered in coastal areas where it is moderately common where not persecuted. Its length is 70-90 cm (Chris Doughty et al., *Birds of the Solomon Islands, Vanuatu and New Caledonia* (London: Christopher Helm, 1999), 56).
133 It is unclear here if Crossan means 'kai kai' or 'kiki'. Kai kai is a common Tok Pisin word for food or feast and can mean 'eat'. 'Kai' is also the Maori word for food and may have been familiar to Crossan from New Zealand. Here 'kiki' apparently signifies a feast or dance during the rituals that marked the end of the yam planting season. In the Arosi language 'hai kiikii' means 'a contest' and 'kookoo' is the name of a dance (Fox, *Arosi Dictionary*, 246, 250).
134 On 5th, 6th and 7th December Crossan's intention had been to sail south-east to Makira Harbour, stating at first that they would leave 'in a day or two' and then 'tomorrow' if the wind was fair. It may be that unfavourable weather made him change his mind, and instead he sailed north to Maro'u Bay which on this occasion supplied him with 7,000 coconuts, sufficient to make almost 1 ton of copra.
135 The home village of this chief or 'King' is not stated, but the reference to 'another outrage committed in the Bush' by 'another mob of bushmen' suggests that this chief came from an inland place. Political relations between coastal and inland peoples could be complex. John Cromar visited Makira Harbour in *Storm Bird* early in 1885, and reported as follows: 'On going ashore I found that my old native friend Taylor, who had a trading store there, had died, and his house was occupied by a chief, Taae by name. This man was not a coastal native, but had come to be chief of the Makira people in a singular manner…. The bush natives were at enmity with the coastal ones at Makira, and had shot dead the latter's chief whose name had been Taae. Instead of making war on the murderer's people, the coastal natives demanded of them a full-blown chief to replace the one who had been killed, and who, having no children, had died without an heir. The bush natives consented to this arrangement, and in due course produced the chief, who forthwith took over Taae's name and chieftainship amidst general rejoicing at such a satisfactory conclusion to a long-standing feud' (Cromar, *Jock of the Islands*, 146-7).

Wednesday 10th Dec 85

Boat went to Morrow bay for Nuts & collect copra from Lohu. Day warm & fine. Came home abt 3 p.m.

Thursday 11th Dec 85

My Birthday[136] tomorrow I presume, rather quiet. Corn beef for Breakfast, Dinner & Tea. Johnstone a little sick this morning, I gave him a good stiff dose of Castor oil, which operated in rather quick time. Day showry southerly wind blowing, a few more gentle shocks of Earthquake (nice company).

Friday 12th 1885 December

Dull day. Johnstone working at house. Luai smoking copra.[137] Bought a little copra today. Anxiously awaiting for wind to go down to Mackeria.

Saturday 13th [December]

Day very warm & fine. Busy smoking copra. Johnstone hard at work at house. Everything quiet, nothing of importance to note. The only book I have got to read now is Henry Georges which is pretty deep.[138]

Sunday 14th [December]

Day warm & fine. Fore & Aft schooner in sight. N.W. breeze blowing, abt 2 p.m. put out for Mackeria, got sight of vessel putting in for Hada Bay. Steered boat for there. The Duro, Capt Peter Sorenson in charge from Houla, put in here to land 2 Boys.[139] Went on board & had a talk with him. He gave me an act of his voyage, and told me the carryings on of Otto Ashe the sailing master, he running away with the boys, boat &etc at the Catarad group, & the detention of the boat & boys by the Germans at Mioko.[140] Some of the boys there engaged

---

136 William Crossan reached the age of 24 on 11th December 1885.
137 'Luai' is possibly an alternative name for 'Lalloa' who is mentioned on 25th December as one of 'the only two natives worth taking notice of here' (the other was Johnstone). In January Lalloa twice supplied Crossan with pigeons that he had shot, to reciprocate perhaps the plum duff that Crossan had given him on Christmas Day.
138 The best-known book by the political economist Henry George is *Progress and Poverty*, which was published in 1879.
139 The exploits of Captain Peter Sorenson of the *Douro* and the role of Otto Ashe and Sam Craig in his exposure are fully described by Laracy ('Niels Peter Sorenson', 147-162). Crossan's account shows how Sorenson and his white crew managed to cover up the facts about the violent and criminal nature of their trading activities in Solomons and the Bismarck Archipelago. Sorenson arrived at Makira from 'Houla', i.e. Aola on the north coast of Guadalcanal.
140 The Carteret group, otherwise known as Kilinailau, is an atoll east of Bougainville. Ashe, two other white men and seven Solomon Islanders sailed from Kilinailau to Mono in the Treasury Group, SE Bougainville, where there was a British Navy coaling station. There they met Sam Craig in the *Princess Louise* who took them to Mioko in German New Guinea, from whence Ashe reached Cooktown, Queensland, where he made a full report on Sorenson's criminal behaviour (Laracy, 'Niels Peter Sorenson', 153).

to work for the Germans & understood it was to be for 2 years, but Sorenson understanding the G language saw that they had engaged for 4 years. He says that he told the Germans not to take the Boys, but to let them come back to the ship to go to their homes. Otto Ashe shot one boy of Bougainville in a canoe, when they had taken the nuts of the island. I read Sorenson's Log up to the time Ashe kept it, and the treatment of King John and what the paper states is in contradiction to one another.[141] What the white men on board say of Sorenson, that he has acted straightforward enough in all his transactions to the natives, and very decently to them. The labour appears quite contented. Intend going to Mackira tomorrow, where the Duoro has to land one boy.

Monday 15th Dec 85

Day warm & fair. Went of to schr Duro & bought some tobacco & sold one ton copra. I am taking one boy back to Mackira for Sorenson, he is left in charge of Johnstone who he origanally belonged to. The schooner intends putting out tomorrow for Cookstown.[142]

Tuesday 16th Dec 85

Day fine no wind, went of to the schr Duoro, & stopped there all day. In the evening Manuma came on board from Lohu & gave a full detailed account of the whole affair from when he joined the ship till he was enticed away by the Master.[143] He gave the statements before all the white crew & Johnstone. It was signed by all hands & delivered to the Captain. Came ashore in the evening, about 5 p.m. No appearance of wind.

---

141   King John was a chief from Wagina island who Sorenson had kidnapped, and ransomed to extort from the islanders beche-de-mer, tortoiseshell and copra (Laracy, 'Niels Peter Sorenson', 152). Crossan is here comparing the information in the ship's log with what he knew about already from reading the Australian press, which began reporting Ashe's allegations about Sorenson in September 1885.
142   'Cookstown' is Cooktown in northern Queensland. Upon his arrival in Cooktown on 24th December 1885 Sorenson was arrested, tried and sentenced to eight years in prison (Laracy, 'Niels Peter Sorenson', 154-5).
143   'Manuma' from Lohu is the same man as the 'Manumua' who took part in the mutiny against Sorenson on the *Douro*. He was therefore one of the group that had sailed in a long boat with Otto Ashe to German Bougainville, was picked up by Sam Craig (Laracy, 'Niels Peter Sorenson', 153), and later was put ashore by him either at Lohu (Rohurua) or at Buna (Ubuna) on 24th November. It would appear that once he was on board the *Douro* again and surrounded by white men, Manuma/Manumua decided that it would be wise for him to apologise for taking part in the mutiny ('he was enticed away by the Master [Otto Ashe]' is Crossan's kind interpretation) and to make a statement supportive of Captain Sorenson and his crew. It is a sign of the looming Pax Britannica that this statement was regarded as important enough to be written down and signed by all the European witnesses and by Johnstone, before being delivered to Captain Sorenson. However, this 'evidence' did not save Sorenson from a jail sentence when he returned to Queensland and certain of his crew decided to testify against him (see footnote to 26th November). By the end of December the statement that Crossan had signed was being widely reproduced in the Australian press (e.g. Seizure for Piracy, *The Brisbane Courier*, 28 December 1885, 5). The statement ends '(signed), Mamu (mark); Johnston, native king (mark); Wm. Crossan, trader; S.D. Llalland; August Thomson; Chas. Leslie; Eugene S. Montague'.

Wednesday 17th Dec 1885

Day fine & warm, light S. breeze blowing. The Duoro put out to sea abt 9 a.m. for Cooktown. Nothing of any importance to note.

Thursday 18th [December]

Day warm & fine. Bought some copra. Johnstone working at house.

Friday 19th [December]

Day warm & fine. Sandy & 3 Boys came from Lunichena to go to Mackeria. Got ready & put out abt 8 a.m., fair wind down, got there abt 4 p.m., landed Boy home from S.S. Duoro. Santa Anna canoes there, 4 of them. They had just killed one Rubiana boy staying at Makeria & sold him to the Boys at Anutua.[144] Slept in the Boat all night.[145] Fine.

Saturday 20th [December]

Day fine. Put in copra. Went to Obau[146] & Waisingho's place, & left trade. Then on to Anutua, where took in copra, and seen the scalp of the departed sticking on a poll. The men brought some of the dead carcase up to eat. Fair wind back, got home abt 6 p.m. very hungry, tired & sunburnt.

Sunday 21st [December]

Day fine & warm. Johnstone working at house. Cut up copra. George went to my Boys house last night & threatened to kill him. I intend to give him a punching with my fists if he puts in his appearance here again.[147]

---

144 On this day Crossan used the 'fair wind' to sail all the way from Hada Bay to Makira Bay. He reports that people from Santa Ana have murdered a man from Rubiana (Roviana Lagoon) in order to make a transaction with villagers from Anuta Island. Roviana is in the western Solomon Islands, and a person from there living on Makira without chiefly or Mission protection would have had few friends to protect him against such opportunistic killing.
145 In view of the murder reported at Makira Harbour, Crossan shows that he is unwilling to risk his life by sleeping ashore and instead stays on board all night to guard his boat, no doubt heavily armed. There was a three-quarters moon that night.
146 'Obau' (probably Apaora) is on the coast south of Makira Harbour. This long trip was accomplished in daylight, but if Crossan had been delayed he could have returned some hours later by moonlight, there being a full moon on 22nd December.
147 This is probably the same George who had made a good plum duff in Crossan's house on 14th September. A month after this fight George was still employed at the Hada station, and was being treated by Crossan for fever (see entry for 30th January), which suggests that Crossan's threat to punch him if he put in another appearance was not effective.

Monday 22nd December 1885

Day fine. Johnstone & his wife are making native money for me.[148] The boys are at Mulhou making a big Kiki.[149] He tells me he don't care for money now, for when he dies he cant take it with him, and if he got sick plenty of the men would come about him, to get it. He is going to throw all he has got in the sea, when he gets sick. This approaches very near our civilisation.

Tuesday 23rd [December]

Day dull & showry, any quantity of thunder & lightning. I think the natives are staunch Roman Catholics. My boys foot is sore & swollen, an old native came to look at it. Got some fresh water in a shell, talked about ½ an hour over it & then put it on his foot & said it would soon be better. The same old Josser has got very bad eyes, & asked me to make him up a lotion to put on them. They are a most superstitious race, & out & out canabials.

Wednesday 24th [December]

Day fine. Steve's Cutter here today from Morau. Wilson came ashore & had a short yarn with him.[150] He is complaining very much abt the slowness of copra coming in. Gave him some Kawais,[151] as he was out of tucker for his men. Christmas Eve in the islands is rather a monotonous time. Boat away at Buna and Heula today, Johnstone in chge. H.M.S [*symbol of diamond*] N. of us, has been in Uigi to snatch the murderer of Adams.[152]

---

148 'Native money' refers to strings of shell money consisting of small discs made from certain shells broken and rubbed into shape, the holes being drilled with a point of flint or obsidian (Codrington, *The Melanesians*, 325). Gifts of shell-money to Europeans happened occasionally. In 1869, for example, when the missionary Joseph Atkin went from Wango into Bauro district on a peace-making trip, he was taken to a chief's house: 'Takana, the chief, met me before the door, and hung a handsome present of native money around my neck' (Halcombe, *Mission Life*, 141). Ivens provides the following summary of the normal uses in Ulawa-Sa'a: 'the shell-money is put to the following uses: the furnishing of the bride-price and the blood-money, the buying of canoes, the payment of fees and fines, including redemptive offerings to ghosts, the buying of pigs and food; single strings of varying lengths are in common use for making purchases' (Ivens, *Melanesians of the South-East Solomons*, 391). In 1923 a man called Monogai from Heuru village told Rev. C.E. Fox that formerly the shell discs were made at U-wai-wara, a place near Parigina on the south coast of Makira, east of the Arosi region, 'but the industry has now ceased' (White, 'The material culture of Makira', 245). Crossan's information for Hada shows that formerly the industry was more widespread.
149 For 'kiki' see footnote to 7th December. This particular feast at Mulhau took place on the night of the full moon.
150 This appears to be the return of the same cutter that departed on 2nd November from Hada Bay to Marau (probably Wawa Marau Island, south of Makira Harbour). Possibly 'Wilson' is John Wilson, an English seaman who killed a trader at Mioko, Duke of York Islands, in a drunken brawl in 1878, and thereafter lived in Solomon Islands as a trader himself, finally working for Lars Nielsen at Gavutu in Nggela between 1891 and 1896 (Golden, *The Early European Settlers*, 144).
151 'Kawai' is the Fijian name for Sweet Yam, *Dioscorea esculenta*, known in Tok Pisin as 'pana'. Crossan's use of the word kawai reflects his former Fijian connections.
152 Crossan provides no details about the murder of G.B. Adams, who was killed near Seragini, close to present-day Pamua when his ship *Lucy Adams* was wrecked on Makira Island in April 1885. Although Adams had once been a seaman on the recruiting vessel *Stanley*, he had not been to Makira before (Clayton to Tryon,

Thursday 25th December 1885

Day warm & fine. Quiet Christmas.[153] Boat back from Buna could take in no copra at Tawatana, owing to the heavy sea running. Steve's cutter beating about of Buna can make no progress with sea & tide. Ned made a duff for Johnstone & Lalloa, they are the only two natives worth taking notice of here. A canoe put in to Buna from Guadalcanar with 10 men, on passing Heula they gave chase, fired 2 or 3 shots, & broke the top of the canoe. That is the way they treat visitors in these parts.

Friday 26th [December]

Day dull & showry. Sandy came from Linuchena and I gave him a duff. Intend going to Morrow Bay tomorrow to smoke copra. Natives all in bush working. Johnstone busy at house.

Saturday 27th [December] 85

Heavy showers fell through the day, nothing of importance to note.

Sunday 28th [December]

Heavy thunder & lightning all day. Natives in bush, everything quiet.

Monday 29th [December]

Day dull. Towards evening very heavy showers fell, wind N.W. Johnstone came to the house this evening. Got over his tiff. The boys came to go in the boat this morning but said nothing about it, and I would not let them see that I was anxious to go. Never submit to a Nigger.[154] All well.

Tuesday 30th Dec 85

Went to Moroo bay with my Boys. Fair wind. Got there abt 10 a.m. Some Lohu boys came to cook copra also. Day fine & warm.

---

28 November, 1886, enclosure, WPHC 33/86, WPA). The screw corvette H.M.S. *Diamond* was described as 'an old full-rigged cruiser with auxiliary power... a stately and imposing old craft' (Douglas Rannie, *My Adventures among South Sea Cannibals* (London: Seeley, Service & C. Ltd., 1912), 241). Based in British Fiji, this ship was active in Solomon Islands waters in 1884-85 investigating murders of British subjects and other outrages (Golden, *The Early European Settlers*, 220, 434).

153 Since Crossan had not corrected the error that he made in his diary on 7th November, he and Ned were celebrating what they thought was Christmas Day on Christmas Eve.

154 This latest 'tiff' involving Johnstone is not fully explained. Crossan's stated intentions on 26th December to leave 'tomorrow' for Maro'u Bay seems to have been frustrated until the 30th, but (apart from bad weather) the reason for delay is unclear.

Wednesday 31st [December]

Morroo Bay. Day fine, men busy cooking copra. Some bush men came down to cook. Looked for turtle in the evening, no success. Got plenty of turtle eggs.

Thursday January 1st 1886

Morroo Bay. Morning dull, got ready for a start. Men cooked abt 4,000 nuts. Got some more copra of my trader at Lohu Otegallio, got home abt 2 p.m. Cut up the copra, feell rather tired.

Friday January 2nd 1886

Very heavy S.W. wind blowing accompanied with squalls.[155] Heavy sea running. Thundered very hard last night. Bought a very nice bird from the Mulhau people this morning. Took boat ashore this afternoon. Bussy smoking copra. Johnstone in good humor again. I wish this wind was over as I could get away to Makira.

Saturday 3 Jany 86

Strong S.W. breeze, toward afternoon very heavy rain squalls passed over. Smoking nuts all day. Mai out shooting pigeons. Fixed up door in Johnstone's house. Big sea running.

Sunday 4th Jany 1886

Very heavy wind & rain all day, thought the house was going to blow away. The sea rose about 2 ft, heavy sea rolling in. Bussy smoking nuts all day. Made the boat more secure.

Monday 5th Jany 1886

Very heavy winds all night. Sea rose abt 3 ft during the day.[156] Still blowing a gale, thought we would have to shift out of the house today. Got the copra & out houses secured. Gave trade to a native today at Moatie.[157]

Tuesday 6th [January]

Morning calm, sea went down during the day to its ordinary level. One of the natives very sick, gave him some medicine. Towards evening he was a little out

---

155 The normal season for westerly squalls in Solomon Islands is December to April, during the warmer and wetter Northwest Monsoon season. Crossan noted on 29th December that the wind had shifted to the north-west.

156 What Crossan describes here are the symptoms of a tropical cyclone generating a 1 metre storm surge in Hada Bay, but without the severe damage that would signal hurricane-force winds.

157 'Moatie' is probably Mwata, a village just 4 km south of Hada Bay.

of his mind & came out on the beach, with his face chenamical[158] & brandishing ½ doz spears. I went over & saw him, they told me had just killed one man, gave him 25 drp of Laudanum.[159]

Wednesday 7th [January]

Morning wet, day turned out fine. Made a trade box[160] & cleaned the rifles. The natives have got a fine lot of young Turtles, which they are going to rear.[161] Wind & sea rose towards evening.

Thursday 8th [January]

Day fine, N.W. breeze blowing, Johnstone working at house, nothing of importance to note.

Friday 9th January 1886

Day fine, fresh N.W. breeze. Johnstone & 2 Boys away to Lohu on foot.

Saturday 10th [January]

Day fine & warm. Jackie came for more trade this morning. Johnstone & Boys came back from Lohu this evening. Wind altered round to S.W.

Sunday 11th [January]

Morning dull, light westerly breeze. Went over & asked Johnstone to get the boys to launch the Boat. After a lot of lingering & persuasion, they came over & launched her. Got all the trade ready & then none of them would go, this put me out, so I stopped all trade here, do not intend to buy any more local Copra, try & bring the swines up with a round turn somehow. Johnstone went away this afternoon to Moatie to get some boys to go to Makira in the morning, came

---

158 By 'chenamical' Crossan means 'covered in *chunam*' or quick-lime, used locally for medicinal purposes (see footnote for 21st September).

159 Laudanum is a tincture of opium in alcohol, and in Victorian times it was widely prescribed as, amongst other things, a soporific. A dose of laudanum was 'equivalent to a grain of opium … thirteen minims, or about 25 drops' (George B. Wood, *Treatise on Therapeutics and Pharmacology or Materia Medica* (Philadelphia: J.B. Lippincott, 1860), 770), so it would seem that Crossan was treating his psychotic patient according to the normal dosage.

160 A trade box was usually a pine chest measuring 36 inches by 18 inches with a lockable lid, and was used by labourers on their return from Queensland (Graves, 'Truck and gifts', 88). Probably the local traders in villages who acted as agents for men like Crossan were supplied with trade boxes, as places to store their tobacco, matches and other goods.

161 The rearing of hawksbill turtles was probably a practice stimulated by the trade in 'tortoiseshell', which was fetching 12 shillings/lb in Sydney at this time. Tortoiseshell had for a long time been traded to whaling ships at Makira Harbour and elsewhere (Bennett, *Wealth of the Solomons*, 52). Almost every trading ship arriving in Sydney from Solomon Islands had a quantity of tortoiseshell in its cargo, but in the 1880s the quantities shipped were much less than in the 1860s, probably because of over-exploitation (Bennett, *Wealth of the Solomons*, 358-361).

back, but all the Boys were at Lunichena.[162] The Bushmen have just killed one Boy belonging to Chief of Lunichena, a return just back from Port McKay.[163] So much for civilized San Christoval, this is no. 4 that has got his quick dispatch, with one white man, in 4 months, that I know of.[164]

Monday 12th [January] 86

Morning fine, S.W. breeze. 4 Bushmen came here this morning, some of the same tribe that killed the boy at Lunichena. I heard that their object for coming was for to declare peace with this place, & exterminate the Lunichena tribe.

The natives brought some Copra here today but I told them to take it away again. This took them down a peg, in the eyes of the Bushmen, when they were talking big to them.[165] Night very fine.

Tuesday 13th January 1886

Day fine & warm S.S.W. breeze. Went to Lunichena after dinner & got some copra from Seua.[166] They were all in fighting trim, had been in bush all day looking for man, they are going to burn a bushman's town tomorrow. As soon as the yam planting is done they do little but fight, always employed.

Wednesday 14th [January]

Day very warm. Johnstone & George away to the native meeting at Lohu. Lalloa out & shot 4 pigeons. Intend going to Linichena in the morning.

---

162   If 'Moatie' is present-day Mwata and 'Lunichena' is somewhere near Rumahui, the men that Johnstone was seeking had travelled about 5 km south to the next big coastal village.
163   This killing of a returned labourer from Port Mackay (Queensland) represents a further episode in the endless series of pay-back killings that seem to have marked relations between Lunichena and inland groups at this time.
164   This death Crossan adds to the four other murders that he had heard about: 19th October 1885 (bushman shot by local trader Sandy of Tawaraha for ceremonial canoe launch), 9th December 1885 (chief killed by bushmen on his way home from trading in Anutua), 19th December 1885 (Roviana man who was living at Makira Harbour killed, corpse sold to Anutua), plus the murder of G.B. Adams, trader, in April 1885. It is significant that all five killings are related in some way to trading or labour recruiting. Crossan seems to discount as more of an accident the reported death at Hada Bay on 6th January 1886, where a man was killed by a lunatic.
165   Crossan's intention here is to humiliate the Hada Bay men in the eyes of the watching bushmen, in order to persuade some to join him on a trading voyage to Makira Harbour following their refusal to go there on 11th January. Since the men's own chief (Johnstone) had failed to find anyone to go to Makira, because of the turmoil following the Lunichena murder, Crossan's strategy appears a little desperate. It was to be another five days before he could persuade his men to make the planned trip.
166   Seua of Lunichena village was also mentioned on 10th January, and is probably the same man as Suedangai (13th October), Seudangi (20th October, 6th December), Swea (21st October), Sewa (26th October), Sewedanga (1st December) and Seudangai (27th January).

Thursday 15th [January]

Day very warm. All the men & woemen away to Lohu. Amused myself catching Butterflies. 2 shocks of earthquake in the afternoon.

Friday 16th [January]

Day very warm. Johnstone & all the Boys back from the meeting. Started for Mackira in the evening, got there abt 3 a.m.[167]

Saturday 17th [January]

Makira. Went to Lehua[168] took in Copra, then into harbour & took in copra there, then Obau & on to Wassinghous'.[169] Rained very hard, which makes boating miserable, got home abt 10 p.m.

Sunday 18 [January]

Emptied Boat, & put the Copra out to dry, got it cut up. Intend going to Buna tonight if weather is fine. Day very warm. Started for Buna 7.30 p.m.

Monday 19th [January]

Aheula, got Copra, also Tawatana, Buna, & Lohu. Beat up to Aheula, got there at daybreak.[170] Two of the Boys had a fight in the Boat, but ended in nothing. Day very warm. Brought up Keilihea from Lohu, took in abt. 2 tons, got home abt 6 p.m.

Tuesday 20th 1886 January

Day fine & warm. Cut up all the copra. Gave trade to Keilihea. Sam's woman very sick, gave her some medicines.[171] Copra came in from Mulhau.

---

167 Crossan was sailing the cutter to Makira Harbour under the light of a half moon. Next day the weather became overcast and wet, making the journey 'miserable'.
168 'Obau' is probably Apaoro near Wawa Marau Island; Lehua is probably Rihu'a just south of Makira Harbour.
169 The identity of 'Wassinghou' is unknown. Crossan went there again for copra on 2nd March 1886.
170 The moon was full on 20th January 1886 and we can infer that the weather had improved on the 18th, both of which made feasible the all-night passage to Ubuna. The cutter then had to beat against the prevailing easterly winds for the final leg from Ubuna to 'Lohu' (Rohurua) and 'Aheula' (Heuru). Heuru is about 8 miles (13 km) beyond Ubuna and was the furthest point east that Crossan ever travelled on this coast.
171 Sam's wife is referred to again three days later, but we are not told the identity of Sam. Three days later there is another reference to sickness (Mai's wife), and it may be that a malaria epidemic had begun in Hada Bay connected to wetter conditions in the North West season – Crossan had been noting wet weather since late December. The incidence of malaria fluctuates seasonally in Solomon Islands (B. Appleyard et al., 'Malaria in pregnancy in the Solomon Islands: barriers to prevention and control', *American Journal of Tropical Medicine and Hygiene* 78 (3), 2008, 449-454).

Wednesday 21st [January]

Went to Morrow Bay, day fine & warm, abt 30 natives from other villages there, got them to collect nuts. Mai shot one pig & they had a big feed, stayed there all night, small boat filled up & came home.

Thursday 22nd [January]

Morning fine, filled up the Big Boat & put out for home. Most of the Boys here away to a meeting in the Bush. Sent trade to Lahea,[172] & Buna. Got home abt 4 p.m.

Friday 23rd [January]

Day dull, heavy showers. Made a door for Johnstone's home. Mai's wife sick, gave her some Medicine. Sam's wife no better.

Saturday 24th [January]

Very heavy thunder last night, & rain. Cutler's Boat put in this morning.[173] I went off with some wine & medicine for the Captain, gave them some kawais, & nuts for the Boys on board.[174]

Sunday 25th [January] 85

Morning wet & miserable. Doing a little Gunsmith work today. Boys bussy smoking copra. Bought a very nice bird of the Parrot species. Johnstone busy working at house.

Monday 26th [January] 1886

Day fine 7 warm. Bussy smoking Copra. Boat going to Anutua in the morning. Boy out & shot some pigeons this afternoon.

Sandy here this morning, selling a fishing canoe. He says there will be no more big wind. The reason he gives is, that the Bushmen, having killed one Boy belonging to his village, that finishes the wind. If the boy had not been killed there would of have plenty of wind. So much for native superstition.

---

172 Lahea is the same trader who was mentioned on 11th November along with his brother. They were probably based in Tawatana to the east of Maro'u Bay.
173 It is unclear who or what 'Cutler's Boat' means, but the captain is obviously a white man in need of wine and medicines. It could possibly be Captain Cuttle, who in 1880 was trading in Solomon Islands waters in a ship called *Maroon*, buying copra, tortoiseshell, ivory nuts, snail shells, etc. (Bennett, *Wealth of the Solomons*, 372-373).
174 'Kawai' is the Fijian word for yam.

Tuesday [January] 27th

Day fine, very heavy tide running from N.W. Small Boat away to Anutua, Johnstone in chge. Bussy smoking Copra all day. Lalloa out & shot 4 pigeons. Jackie came down with his gun to fix this afternoon. Natives preparing for the Bushman tomorrow. Gave Seudangai more trade this afternoon, also Lingie.

Wednesday [January] 28th

Day very warm, bussy drying Copra, all hands away to Hada to meet the Bushmen. Intend going down the coast in the morning for Copra. Ned a little sick.[175]

Thursday [January] 29th

Morning fine. Got up & made a drink of Tea. Ned sick. Took the 3 boats to Harning Eye[176] for nuts, got some more from Lunichena, got back abt sundown. Ned a little better. Jim & Lo busy smoking Copra all day, got abt 2,000.

Friday January 30th 1886

Morning warm, very wet in afternoon. Busy smoking Copra. Took both boats ashore & scrubbed them. Ned very sick. George bad with fever, gave him some medicine.

Saturday 31st [January]

Day showry. Johnstone's Boat went to Lohu for Trade. Busy smoking Copra, & fixing boat. Lingie brought some copra in today. Ned much better also George.

Sunday February 1st

Day fine, doing a little to the Boat. Boys busy smoking Copra. Jackie and his boy down for more tobacco today. Small boat going to Lohu in morning.

Monday 2nd [February]

Day wet & showry. Boat away to Lohu, brought back 1,000. Bussy smoking copra. Ned a little better.

---

175 Surprisingly, this is only the third reference in the journal to Crossan's partner Ned (Edward Griffiths), who arrived on the schooner of 29th October and came ashore on 31st October. Ned made a fire place on 2nd November and a plum duff on Christmas Day, but otherwise his presence is invisible. It seems that it was Crossan who made the trading voyages Maro'u Bay, Ubuna, Makira Harbour, etc. while Ned stayed at Hada Bay and kept the trade store going.

176 'Harning Eye' is probably Harani'ia or Cape Achard, on the south-west point of Makira island. This is the first reference to 'three boats', presumably the small whaleboat, the new sailing cutter, and another one, possibly belonging to Johnstone.

Tuesday 3rd [February]

Day warm. Smoking & cutting up Copra. Ned shot one pig for Dancing. Painted the Boat, paid £. Johnstone painted his Canoe. Lingie brought in some copra today.

Wednesday 4th [February]

Day warm & showry. Done a little to the boats. Johnstone put up some leaves to keep rain out of copra shed.

Thursday 5th [February]

Day warm and fine. Brigantine Helena in sight.[177] Boats working up the shore came here abt 10 a.m. Govt. A. & McKepple mate.[178] Capt. Turner in chge from Maryborough. 40 recruits, & returns to land in Maylata, was in company with Glencairn in Maula[179] in January, & she put out for Maylata, to land returns. Capt Cline in chge, Mr Pilkington G.A.[180] Helena 7 weeks out from Bundaberg.

---

177 John Cromar (*Jock of the Islands*, 203) was the labour recruiter on board *Helena*, and he describes her arrival from Santo, New Hebrides, as follows: 'We saw no land again until we reached the Solomon Islands, where we anchored at Hada Bay in the island of San Cristobal. Here we took in wood and water, and purchased a supply of pannas and bananas from the natives'. While visiting the house of the chief, who he calls 'Johnson', Cromar noticed 'a brand-new Winchester repeating rifle... [Johnstone] had told me on a previous occasion that he intended letting a white man have his two daughters in exchange for a good rifle, but as they still remained at home, it seemed he had made some other deal or arrangement to obtain the weapon.' It was probably Crossan's Winchester that Cromar saw in the house of Johnson/Johnstone, either given to him or on loan. After Crossan left Makira, Johnstone's daughters eventually established some liaison with the traders Dabelle who were French. Tom Dabelle, one of the two brothers, may also have given Johnstone a rifle, as the British warships had no control over non-British subjects trading in arms. Whatever its source, Johnstone put his Winchester to good effect when he heard about a planned raid by Malaitans to steal porpoise teeth, for he organised and led a highly effective ambush, killing most of the 70 raiders. He subsequently displayed their severed heads to Cromar who acquired one of the skulls as a souvenir (Cromar, *Jock of the Islands*, 203-4, 253-255, 277-278).

178 This entry suggests that the Government Agent of the *Helena* and the Mate Mr McKepple came ashore from a ship's boat 'working up the shore' at 10 a.m. It is implied that Crossan later went aboard and left *Helena* at 5 p.m., having talked to Captain Turner and learnt that the *Helena*'s next destination was Port Adam in south Malaita (Crossan's 'Maylata'). Crossan is not named by the *Helena*'s recruiter John Cromar, but in other respects his account matches Crossan's except that Cromar names the Government Agent as 'Mr McKay' not Mr McKepple (Cromar, *Jock of the Islands*, 203-207).

179 Probably Malo Island in the New Hebrides. From Cromar's account (*Jock of the Islands*, 168) we know that the *Helena* certainly anchored at Malo and had been recruiting there for a few days.

180 Two different ships are here being described. It appears that *Helena* had met the *Glencairn* at 'Maula' (Malo Island, New Hebrides?) in January, the latter ship being under Captain 'Cline' (Clyne) with Mr G. Pilkington as Government Agent (see footnote for 24th October). Both the *Helena* and the *Glencairn* were heading for Malaita to return labour. Crossan is intensely interested in the *Glencairn* as it is a ship chartered by his own company, and therefore he awaits its arrival so that he can ship out copra. Crossan himself was intending to return to Fiji or New Zealand when the *Glencairn* next arrived at Hada Bay, an event signalled by the abrupt termination of this diary on 5th March 1886 (G. Pilkington, Journal of *Glencairn*, No. 58, 30 December 1885-14 April 1886, NAF).

Capt. Turner very sick, complaining of his chest,[181] very unfavourable winds, had a heavy blow in the Hebrides, told us of a trader having been killed in the Hebrides, named Craig.[182] Left the ship at 5 p.m. she laying over for Maylata Pt. Adam's.[183] Got 2 bottles of Rum from the Captain.

Friday 6th Feby 86

Day dull. Heavy showers fell in the afternoon. Nothing of importance to note. Expecting to see the Glencairn put in an appearance every time I look out.

Saturday 7th [February]

Day dull, sea rolling in a little heavy, must have been a gale to the W. Bushmen down with copra today. Johnstone in bush & killed one wild pig. Lingie brought in 2,000 copra today.

Sunday 8th [February]

Day dull but warm, every thing very quite. Some bushmen came in the evening with some copra. Reading most of the day. Boy out & shot some pigeons.

Monday 9th February

Day warm & fine. Done a little to the Boat. Abt 11 a.m. 100 Bushmen came down on a friendly meeting although the natives here were very frightened of them, and some talked of taking the bush. I acted cautious with them myself, & would only allow one or two into the House at once. Ned taken sick again with fever today.

Tuesday 10th Feby 86

Day warm & showry. No native visits today. Fine sky in the evening. Has every appearance of the weather taking up S.W. breeze.[184]

---

181 Cromar (*Jock of the Islands*, 228) records that Captain Turner 'fell ill' after the *Helena*'s return to Bundaberg, and was replaced by Captain Weston for the vessel's next voyage.
182 George Craig was a trader based on Epi in the New Hebrides: 'Craig ... was killed on Ambryn in 1885; he had bought copra from another trader, who had left it in charge of a village, and was trying to collect it when the people attacked him, in defence, so they thought, of the other man's property' (Scarr, *Fragments of Empire*, 172; Rannie, *My Adventures*, 87-88). George Craig is not to be confused with Sam Craig, the Solomon Islands trader who Crossan had come close to meeting on 24th November.
183 The fact that the *Helena* stayed for less than one day in Hada Bay suggests that the porpoise drive described by Cromar (*Jock of the Islands*, 204-205) as occurring during this visit in fact took place on a different occasion, possibly a year later when Cromar visited Hada Bay for several days on the *Fearless* and again met Johnstone/Johnson (Cromar, *Jock of the Islands*, 252). Alternatively Cromar's porpoise drive may not have happened in Hada Bay at all. Joseph Dickinson who traded around Makira Island from 1908-26 stated that 'The little harbour of Anuta and its people was important to the whole of the island, for it was here that much of San Cristoval's wealth originated in the form of porpoise teeth, a drive of which I have witnessed on two occasions' (Dickinson, *A Trader in the Savage Solomons*, 59).
184 A southwesterly breeze would have been very unfavourable for the passage of *Glencairn* from Malaita. Crossan makes a daily note of wind directions probably with this in mind. Persistent westerly and southwesterly winds forced the *Glencairn* to take shelter in the lee of Malaita for almost two weeks, before the schooner managed to make Hada Bay on 25th February.

Wednesday 11th [February]

Day warm & fine, small boat went to Linechuna & Tawai to bring in Copra. Northerly wind blowing. Ned very bad with fever again, intend shaping for Makira.[185] Johnstones boat away to Morrow Bay, boys smoking copra there.

Thursday 12th [February]

Day fine & warm. Cut up Copra, & washed out boats. Ned still a little sick. Some bushmen came down in the evening.

Friday 13th [February]

Day fine & warm. Spent the day doing nothing. Luinchena Chief here today. Canoes & Boat home from Morrow Bay in evening with Copra.

Saturday 14th [February]

Day showry. Northerly breeze blowing. Local boys brought in a good lot of copra this morning. Jim busy smoking some more. Made some good bread today.

Sunday 15th February 1886

Showry & windy. Lingie brought down 400 Copra. Some Boys from up the coast came here this morning.

Monday 16th Feby

Strong N.W. breeze blowing. Had to take up Boats. Sea rose very high, can do nothing this weather, & it is a very hard matter to kill time.

Tuesday 17th [February]

Strong N.W. breeze all night, & still blowing. Mended Johnstone's canoe, & done some stone fencing for abt 20 minutes. Bought a little local Copra.

Wednesday 18th [February]

Still blowing. Done a days work at stone fencing, with Johnstone & Jim. All the boys away to the bush for a big feed.[186]

---

185 The intended trip to Makira Bay could not take place for another two weeks because of continued unfavourable weather.
186 This reference to 'a big feed' necessitating the absence of coastal men for at least two days suggests that coast-inland relations were not entirely hostile, or perhaps that the bush people's peace overtures that Crossan mentioned on 12th January were being reciprocated. The feast coincided with a full moon on the night of 18th February 1886.

Thursday 19th [February]

Breeze light, day warm. Village empty of natives.

Friday 20th [February]

Day fine, light N.W. breeze. Had 5 boys bussy fencing. Men home from Bush this afternoon.

Saturday 21st [February]

Very squaly during night. Light N.W. breeze blowing all day. Trying to learn the Gala language.[187] Johnstone bussy fixing up fence. Shot a crain today with the Winchester, it rather surprised the Boys.

Sunday 22nd Feby 1886

Wind altered to S.S.W., fine sunset in evening. Ned had an encounter with a dog in the yard last night, gave him a beating with a stick. Trying to comprehend the native language.

Monday 23rd [February]

Fine day, N.W. breeze, lighter. Bussy this morning taking up roots. After dinner baked some bread. Ned very sick. After tea sighted a schooner witch I take to be the Glencairn & so it is.

Tuesday 24th [February] 86

Fine day, breeze S.S.W.[188] No appearance of schooner. In afternoon sail was sighted, by canoe. Put out to Hada Bay but could see nothing of it, returned disgusted. Think it must be Capt Marryatts Phantom Ship.[189]

Wednesday 25th [February]

Fine day, S.W. breeze. Bussy in the garden. Schooner in sight. After Dinner put out to Morrow Bay, got a sight of her, & then she stood out for Malayta.[190] Came home disgusted, this is my last trip after any vessel.[191]

---

187 The language of the northwest part of Makira island is Arosi. The name 'Gala' is obscure. It could refer to Nggela, but there seems no reason for Crossan to learn this language. According to Fox (*Arosi Dictionary*, 241) the Arosi word for parrot is 'gara', which may not be a coincidence.

188 The fact that Crossan has underlined the change of wind direction to south-southwest indicates his growing impatience over the non-arrival of the *Glencairn*, which he has been expecting to arrive from Malaita since 6th February. Any wind from the south-west would make the passage from Malaita to Hada Bay more difficult.

189 A joking reference to the popular novel *The Phantom Ship* (1839) by Captain John Marryat.

190 We know from the Government Agent's journal that the reason for the *Glencairn*'s departure was that the captain decided that the Hada Bay anchorage was not secure (G. Pilkington, Journal of *Glencairn*, No. 58, 30 December 1885-14 April 1886, NAF).

191 Crossan is now anxious to leave the Solomons. There is no mention in his diary of the incident that Crossan reported to the Government Agent, Pilkington, when he came aboard *Glencairn* in Hada Bay. He stated

Thurday 26th [February]

Day fine. Sighted schooner, went out & met her, went on to Makira with her. Sent Boat with Johnstone, out all night.[192]

Friday 27th [February]

Anchored in Makira in morning. All well.

Saturday 28th

Mackira Bay. Ship painted & sundrie jobs done about her.

March 1st 1886

Went on to Anutua & brought in Copra.[193] Got back abt 9 p.m.

March 2nd Monday

Makira. Went on to Ruatasi, & got Copra of Wassinghow. Then on to Obau, & got Copra there.[194]

March 3rd Tuesday

Went on to Lehua & bought 2 tons Copra of Jack[195] & collected my own produce. Took in Dicks & Wylippies.[196]

---

that on about 25th January his hut keeper E. Griffiths (Ned referred to earlier) had shot a 'boy' through the cheek, and had done so, it seemed, 'without any sufficient provocation' (G. Pilkington, Journal of *Glencairn*, No. 58, 30 December 1885-14 April 1886, NAF). Griffiths was 'very sick' on 30th January, and his illness, almost certainly malaria, may have made him tetchy and perhaps clouded his judgement. We can only speculate why Crossan failed to record anything in his diary about this case, but it may be his awareness of the incriminating nature of written evidence should Griffiths subsequently be accused of manslaughter or murder. For all that, one or other of the Hada Bay traders must have given details to the Government Agent, Pilkington, as he reported it to the immigration authority in Fiji (Acting Agent of Immigration to Secretary of High Commission, 18 May 1886, WPHC 79/86, WPA). It was not until November that H.M.S. *Diamond* arrived in Hada Bay to investigate 'the case of a white trader, who was alleged to have shot a native boy in the cheek … but as the trader had disappeared he could not be punished'. The captain, Clayton gave 'presents' to the boy concerned and the 'chief' by way of compensation, a gesture well understood by Melanesians (The Cruise of H.M.S. Diamond, *The Argus* (Melbourne), 5 January 1887, 10).

192   This entry shows that Crossan now trusted Johnstone to sail the cutter at night by himself while Crossan travelled in comfort on *Glencairn*. The cutter was needed in Makira Harbour for loading Crossan's copra on to *Glencairn*.

193   It seems likely that *Glencairn* remained at anchor in Makira Harbour while Crossan and Johnstone sailed to Anutua (Anuta Island) in the Hada Bay cutter, returning about 9 p.m. to the *Glencairn*. This was prudent as Anuta Island had no anchorage for a large vessel (Hand to Fairfax, 10 July 1889, WPHC 191/1889, WPA).

194   The exact location of Ruatasi is not known. Obau is probably the village of Apaora near Wawa Marau island, south of Makira Harbour.

195   This 'Jack' has amassed a useful quantity of copra, 2 tons being worth about £15 on the beach. He may be the same person who was on board the *Young Dick* on 16th November, having just returned from Maryborough, Queensland. It is unclear if Jack is a European or a Makira islander, but whether he is one or two persons this 'Jack' should not be confused with 'Jackie', the name that Crossan gives to a local trader who lived not far from Hada Bay and visited Crossan there on three occasions.

196   The identities of 'Dick' and 'Wylippie' are not known.

Wednesday 4th [March] 86

Makira, left there abt 7 p.m. & got in to Mata abt 2 p.m.[197] Took of 3 Boats of Copra, & sent lot of goods ashore. All well at home.[198]

Thursday 5th [March] 1886[199]

---

197   It is not clear if Crossan means 7 p.m. the previous evening, or whether '7 p.m.' is actually an error for '7 a.m.'. According to the Government Agent the *Glencairn* arrived at Hada about 3.30 p.m. and then landed stores and trade and loaded copra (G. Pilkington, Journal of *Glencairn*, No. 58, 30 December 1885-14 April 1886, NAF).
198   When Crossan says 'all well at home' he probably means that all is well at Hada Bay, his home for the past seven months, and that Ned Griffiths has not become the victim of retaliation after the shooting incident of the previous week. Mata is Mwata, a village only 5 km south of Hada Bay, so within reach of news sent by Ned, who as usual had remained at the station.
199   The actual day the diary ended was Thursday 4th March not 'Thursday 5th March', as Crossan had never corrected the error that he first made on 7th November. No other diary entries follow the last (incorrect) date that he wrote, and the following page in the exercise book is blank. It seems reasonable to conjecture that in the rush of loading copra from Hada Bay, packing up his belongings and leaving, Crossan put aside the diary and it was never completed. With the possible exception of some scribblings and words in a child's hand on a later page, there is no evidence that the notebook was ever used again. Pilkington's journal tells us that Crossan departed from Hada Bay on 5th March, after the *Glencairn* had been to Uki and back. He and E. Griffiths came on board as passengers for Auckland. The unnamed 'boy' whom Griffiths had shot had healed and was 'quite recovered', Pilkington reports. It seems likely that someone else, possibly Baker, took over the Hada Bay station. The *Glencairn* went first to the New Hebrides to return labourers, before reaching New Zealand. It anchored off Railway Wharf in Auckland at noon on 14th April and by mid-May was back again in Fiji (G. Pilkington, Journal of *Glencairn*, No. 58, 30 December 1885-14 April 1886, NAF).

Appendix 1. 'My Dearest Aunt'

This is a transcript of the draft of the letter that was written by Crossan in the first few pages of the notebook that he later used as a diary. It was drafted in Clinton, Otago, in 'the second month of spring', in other words probably in October 1881. His aunt was resident in Victoria, Australia. It is likely that this woman was his mother's sister as he mentions her care for him as an infant, possibly after the sudden death of his father.

Clinton 1881

My Dearest Aunt,

For the first time during my sojourn in life I take the greatest pleasure in writing you this letter at my Dear Mothers request. I have been going to write you a letter several times but some how or other I could never make up my mind to do so thinking to myself that I could not compose a letter good enough to send over the waters. although never succeeding seeing you, by what Dear Mother tells me you have seen me and nursed me but those days are out of recollection. I have seen your letters in our album and also that of my Uncle and my Dear Cousin Clementine.

When you see the address at the top of the letter you will see I am not living at home I am 70 miles further down south in a small & rising township called Clinton the centre of what promises to be a great farming district in the future. It is all a newly settled country this where I am. But where my people are it is of a more civilised appearance. Father is not in Tottomairiro [*Tokomairiro district*] just now although we have a place of Business there which is leased to a man that was working for us for 15 years. Tottomairiro as regards business at the present time is very quiet but in Berwick that is the name where Father has his Business just now is also a thriving place and they have a very nice property there and a very good Business in the way of Draper Grocer Baker & everything you can think of one has got to turn their hand too to get on in New Zealand

I believe it is a very fine climate in Victoria rather to warm sometimes as it is too cold her [*sic*] occasionally but this is a very healthy climate & a very productive country in the way of Grain, Sheep & Cattle, wool and Dairy Products. In fact Dairy Produce is a complete Pest in the summer time no market for it here at all and in Country Storekeeping it comprises the cheaf [sic] feature in the trade to do anything like a business you must go into it. Business in N.Z. has been at an utter stagnation for these last 4 years but it is beginning to revive again.

I got my Photo taken to send you over one but I have left them at home and I will write and tell Mother to send you one if she has not sent you one before this time as she kept one to send over to you. But if they are all away I will get them takin [sic] shortly again I wont forget to send one them

At the present time when I am writing this long epistle there is snow lying on the ground 6 inchs [sic] deep although it is the second month of spring – but we often have our worst weather in the spring season. The winter here has been a good one. Dear Mother is in the very best of health as she generally is she is a perfect wonder if you only knew what she manages to do. She is the main stay of Father's Business always at the Books and a very correct Bookeeper [sic] too. My eldest sister Agnes is of some help to Mother now very good in the house as does principally all the cooking & makes herself generally usefull in the Store at times Agnes & Johny was up the Country some time ago on a trip to their grandpapas & their uncles the [sic] live a long way up the Country at the Tiviot [Teviot] All my uncles are Farmers some of them on a large scale & go in for making money. Elizabeth that the name of my second sister she is pretty useful to Mother now & Richard he is the smart one on the family list he is going to be a clever lad he is all there for riding horses he is quiet [sic] an expert at it and as we have plenty of horses Dick makes very good use of them always taking care to give the riding ones plenty of exercise He goes out coursing hares with the grey hounds sometimes with Jack & always succeeds in getting some. Hares are very plentiful here and Game of all sorts

Margaret and Mary are the two youngsters of the family. Maggie and myself are supposed to be the very image of our Mother. Maggie is quiet [sic] a little chatterbox. She would make you laugh if you only heard her sometimes. As for myself I have mentioned before in the letter I am now at Clinton. I am Head Storman [sic] for Robert Scobie a large Storkeeper [sic] up here. I thought in my mind I would take a short trip from home for a shortish time to see what the world is like and I am getting on fine.

It is the first situation ever I was at in my life but I am pretty well up in the Storekeeping Business. I am going to make it my profession. I get a very good salary £150 - - a year with a Bonus of £20 - - at the end of my term with Board & Loding [sic] & I can make myself pretty comfortable out of that. I will be 20 years of age on the 11th Day of December 1881

Appendix 1. 'My Dearest Aunt'

that is my Birthday and by the next Birthday if I am spared me and Dear Mother will be in Melbourne for a short stay to see you if all goes well as I hope it will. It is Mothers greatest wish to see you. She is always talking of taking a trip. But really I dont know how she will manage to get away but we will make some arrangements for the long talked of trip by that time. As this is my first attempt to write such a long letter as this I must draw to a conclusion. You can expect to get one of my photos as soon as I get them taken hoping this will reach its destination in due course of time. And in return I expect [*one line left blank*] and also a few words from my Dear Cousin Clementine and I will be only to glad to pay attention and correspond back to it again. With kindest love dear Aunt & Uncle & the remainder of the family, hoping you are all in excellent health and enjoying the pleasures of this life.

I remain

Your loving & ever remembering Nephew

William Crossan

Adress c/o

    Robert Scobie

    Merchant

    Cluto

    Otago

    New Zealand

Appendix 2. 'All goods at the time of arrival…'

This is an untitled and undated statement written by Crossan on the last few pages of the notebook. The phrase 'To your Master tell everything at the time of occurrence' suggests that this checklist dates from the time when Crossan was working as storeman for Robert Scobie of Clinton, Otago, i.e. the period 1881–83, rather than his later period as an independent storekeeper. The list or creed seems to be based on the kind of material to be found in contemporary manuals of business etiquette such as M. C. Dunbar's *Complete handbook of etiquette: Clear and concise directions for correct manners,* New York: Excelsior, 1884.

All goods at the time of arrival should be chequed marked without delay

Keep your books well posted up & your a/c to your customers regular, long credit is a bad principall. Never do a Business with Single Men. Take men of little standing for your customers & let them be chosen ones if possible

Be punctual in your payments

Never deceive your Banker once deceived he will never trust you again

Take care of the small things & the large ones in due course of time will take care of them selves

Keep away from Whiskey during Business hours when Business is done then indulge if you have a mind but never let yourself crave after it

Stick to the Church & get the good opinion of People with whom among you dwell. When you promise always fulfil. A liar must have a good recoletion [*sic*] & often sets a snare for himself and is entrapped in it. Never get into too many spes [*speculations?*] at a time look after what you have got.

Profitable. On quick sale Cumberland [*meaning obscure*]

Be thankfull God --- work and live

Never in Business put of for a time what you can do at the present moment.

To your Master tell everything at the time of ocurrence [*sic*]

Civility costs nothing. Your business strictly kept to yourself never let anyone know more than they should know. Familiarity as a rule breeds contempt. Keep out of Hotels. Act honestly & think before you speak. Never to go into anything to rashly before you consult men of better judgement than yourself.

Never promises & not fulfil. Always stick to the Truth & shame the Devil. Keep everybody at their distance. Stick to your desk. Always as regards your person spriseness [sic] & neatness one is often judged by your Demeanour. Never cry Poor. Do what you are told & at once & act accordingly.

Let your Customers know at once your mind. Be strict & carefull in money matters.

Never let your expenses outstrip your income.

William Crossan

References

Published maps, books and articles

Admiralty. 1864. *Plan 209, South West Pacific, Anchorages in the Solomon Islands*. London: British Admiralty.

Appleyard, B., Tuni, M., Cheng, Q., Chen, N., Bryan, J. and McCarthy, J.S. 2008. Malaria in pregnancy in the Solomon Islands: barriers to prevention and control. *American Journal of Tropical Medicine and Hygiene* 78(3): 449-454.

Bennett, Judith A. 1987. *Wealth of the Solomons. A History of a Pacific Archipelago, 1800-1978*. Honolulu: University of Hawaii Press.

Biskup, Peter, ed. 1974. *The New Guinea Memoirs of Jean Baptiste Octave Mouton*, Canberra: The Australian National University.

Blain, Michael. 2008. The Blain Biographical Directory of Anglican Clergy in the Pacific. Entries for Comins and Fox. http://anglicanhistory.org.nz/blain_directory.pdf website accessed October 2008.

Brenchley, Julius L. 1873. *Jottings during the Cruise of H.M.S. Curaçoa among the Islands of the South Seas*. London: Longman, Green & Co.

Brooke, C.H. 1873. Progress of the Melanesian Mission. *Mission Life* 4: 440-448. http://anglicanhistory.org/oceania/brooke_progress1873.html website accessed January 2011.

Codrington, R.H. 1885. *The Melanesian Languages*. Oxford: Clarendon Press.

Codrington, R.H. 1891. *The Melanesians*. Oxford: Clarendon Press

Corris, Peter. 1973. *Passage, Port and Plantation. A History of Solomon Islands Labour Migration 1870-1914*. Melbourne: Melbourne University Press.

Cromar, John. 1935. *Jock of the Islands*. London: Faber & Faber.

Crossan, G.S. 1993. *A Baker's Dozen: A History of the Crossan Family and Descendents from 1792-1993*. Dunedin [?], New Zealand, privately printed.

Cyclopedia of Fiji. 1907. Sydney: The Cyclopedia Company of Fiji. Reprinted by Fiji Museum, Suva, 1984.

Diamond, Jared. 1997. *Guns, Germs and Steel. A Short History of Everybody for the Last 13,000 Years*. London: Jonathan Cape.

Doughty, Chris, Day, N. and Plant, A. 1999. *Birds of the Solomons, Vanuatu & New Caledonia*. London: Christopher Helm.

d'Ozouville, Brigitte. 1997. F. H. Dufty in Fiji, 1871-92: The Social Role of the Colonial Photographer in Fiji. *History of Photography* 21(1): 32-41.

Dunbar, M.C. 1884. *Complete Handbook of Etiquette: Clear and Concise Directions for Correct Manners*. New York: Excelsior.

Encyclopaedia of Australian Shipwrecks & Other Maritime Incidents. 2006. Oceans Enterprises, Yarram, Victoria. http://oceansl.customer.netspace.net.au/qld-main.html website accessed October 2008.

Firth, Stewart. 1972. German Firms in the Pacific Islands, 1857-1914. In *Germany in the Pacific and Far East, 1870-1914*, ed. J. A. Moses and P. M. Kennedy, 3-25. St Lucia: University of Queensland Press.

Foljambe, C., Earl of Liverpool. 1868. *Three Years on the Australia Station*. 187 Piccadilly, London: Hatchard & Co., for private circulation. http://www.enzb.auckland.ac.nz/document?wid=2224&p=1

Fox, Charles E. 1924. *The Threshold of the Pacific: a Account of the Social Organisation, Magic and Religion of the People of San Cristoval in the Solomon Islands*. London: Kegan Paul, Trench, Trubner.

Fox, Charles E. 1958. *Lord of the Southern Isles, being the Story of the Anglican Mission in Melanesia 1849-1949*. London: A.R. Mowbray.

Fox, Charles E. 1978. *Arosi Dictionary, Revised Edition with English-Arosi Index prepared by Mary Craft*. Pacific Linguistics, Series C, 57. Canberra: Research School of Pacific Studies, The Australian National University.

Golden, Graeme A. 1993. *The Early European Settlers of the Solomon Islands*. Mentone, Melbourne, privately printed.

Graves, Adrian. 1983. Truck and gifts: Melanesian immigrants and the trade box system in colonial Queensland. *Past and Present* 101: 87-124.

Green, Kaye C. 1976. A history of post-Spanish European contact in the Eastern District before 1939. In *Southeast Solomon Islands Cultural History. A Preliminary Survey,* Bulletin 11, ed. R.C. Green and M. Cresswell, 31-46. Bulletin 11. Wellington: Royal Society of New Zealand.

Guppy, Henry B. 1887. *The Solomon Islands and their Natives*. London: Swan Sonneschein.

Halcombe, Rev. J.J. 1872. *Mission Life: An Illustrated Magazine of Home and Foreign Church Work*. London: W. Wells Gardner. Reprinted by Project Canterbury, http://anglicanhistory.org/oceania/halcombe_atkin1872.html website accessed 29 January 2011.

Herr, R.A. and Rood, E.A., eds. 1978 *A Solomons Sojourn: J.E. Philp's Log of the Makira 1912-1913*. Hobart: Tasmanian Historical Research Association.

Hilliard, David. 1978. *God's Gentlemen: A History of the Melanesian Mission, 1849-1902*. St Lucia, Queensland: University of Queensland Press.

Ioane, Patere [John Craddock]. 1993. *Kanaka Marau. A Socio-Political Drama about the Economy of a Colony 1899-1902*. St Joseph's School, Tenaru, Solomon Islands (privately printed).

Ivens, Walter G. 1927. *Melanesians of the South-east Solomons*. London: Kegan Paul, Trench, Trubner & Co.

Krämer-Bannow, Elisabeth. 2009. *Among the Art-Loving Cannibals of the South Seas*. Trans. Waltraud Schmidt. Adelaide: Crawford House.

Laracy, Hugh. 1976. *Marists and Melanesians. A History of Catholic Missions in the Solomon Islands*. Canberra: Australian National University Press.

Laracy, Hugh. 2000. Niels Peter Sorenson: the story of a criminal adventurer. *Journal of Pacific History* 35: 147-162.

McLean, Mervyn. 1999. *Weavers of Song: Polynesian Music and Dance*. Auckland: Auckland University Press.

Mann, Paul and Taira, Asahiko. 2004. Global tectonic significance of the Solomon Islands and Ontong Java Plateau convergence zone. *Tectonophysics* 389: 137-190.

Munro, Doug. 1987. The lives and times of resident traders in Tuvalu: An exercise in history from below. *Pacific Studies* 10 (2): 73-106.

Muspratt, Eric. 1931. *My South Sea Island*. New York: W. Morrow & Co.

Nunn, Patrick, Heorake, T., Tegu, E., Oloni, B., Simeon, K., Wini, L., Usuramo, S. and Geraghty, P. 2006. Geohazards revealed by myths in the Pacific: a study of islands that have disappeared in Solomon Islands. *South Pacific Studies* 27: 37-49.

Olssen, Erik and Stenson, Marcia. 1990. *A Century of Change: New Zealand 1800-1900*. Auckland: Longman Paul.

Oxford English Dictionary, 2012. http://www.oed.com/ website accessed August 2012.

Pirie, Peter. 1972. The effects of treponematosis and gonorrhoea on the populations of the Pacific Islands. *Human Biology in Oceania* 1(3): 187-206.

Redlich, Edwin. 1874. Notes on the western islands of the Pacific Ocean and New Guinea. *Journal of the Royal Geographical Society* 44: 30-37.

Rietmann, O. 1868. *Wanderungen in Australien und Polynesien*. St Gallen: Scheitlin & Zollikofer.

Ross, Angus. 1964. *New Zealand's Aspirations in the Pacific in the Nineteenth Century*. Oxford: Clarendon Press.

Scarr, Deryck. 1968. *Fragments of Empire. A History of the Western Pacific High Commission 1877-1914*. Canberra: Australian National University Press, Canberra, and Honolulu: University of Hawaii Press.

Scott, Michael. 2007. *The Severed Snake: Matrilineages, Making Place, and a Melanesian Christianity in Southeast Solomon Islands.*, Durham, North Carolina: Carolina Academic Press.

Shineberg, Dorothy, ed. 1971. *The trading voyages of Andrew Cheyne 1841-1844*, Canberra: Australian National University Press.

Tetens, Alfred. 1958. *Among the Savages of the South Seas: Memoirs of Micronesia, 1862-1868*. Trans. Florence Mann Spoehr, Stanford: Stanford University Press.

Thomas, Nicholas and Richard Eves, eds. 1999. *Bad Colonists: The South Seas Letters of Vernon Lee Walker and Louis Becke*. Durham and London: Duke University Press.

Thompson, R.B.M. and Pudsey-Dawson, P.A. 1958. The geology on Eastern San Christoval, 1955-56. In *Memoir, Geological Survey of the British Solomon Islands* ed. John C. Grover, 90-95. London: Crown Agents.

Wawn, William. 1893. *The South Sea Islanders and the Queensland Labour Trade: a Record of Voyages and Experiences in the Western Pacific, from 1875 to 1891*. Ed. Peter Corris, Reprint Canberra: The Australian National University, 1973.

White, Moira. 2007. The material culture of Makira. In *Vastly Ingenious. The Archaeology of Pacific Material Culture, in Honour of Janet M. Davidson*, ed. Atholl Anderson, K. Green and F. Leach, 243-262. Dunedin: Otago University Press.

Wood, George B. 1860. *A Treatise on Therapeutics, and Pharmacology or Materia Medica*, 2 vols. London: B. Lippincott & Co, Philadelphia, and Trubner & Co.

Woodford, Charles M. 1888. Exploration of the Solomon Islands. *Proceedings of the Royal Geographical Society* 10: 351-376.

Woodford, Charles M. 1890. *A Naturalist among the Head-Hunters: being an Account of Three Visits to the Solomon Islands in the Years 1886, 1887 and 1888*. London: George Philip & Sons.

Yen, Douglas E. 1976. Agricultural systems and prehistory in the Solomon Islands. In *Southeast Solomon Islands Cultural History. A Preliminary Survey*. Bulletin 11, ed. R.C. Green, R.C. and M. Cresswell, 61-74. Wellington: Royal Society of New Zealand.

www.ingramcontent.com/pod-product-compliance
Lightning Source LLC
Chambersburg PA
CBHW060947170426
43197CB00031B/2994